Praise for *Is the Commission Still Great?*

To reach the ends of the earth we will need to be informed, encouraged, and engaged with the opportunities before us in this late hour of God's story of redemption. My friend Steve Richardson has written a beautiful book that I believe will stir your heart, remind you what is possible, and fan into flame your love for the nations. The Commission truly is great.

MATT CHANDLER
Lead Pastor, The Village Church

In the recent past, many false assumptions about our responsibility to reach the nations with the good news of Jesus Christ have quietly crept into our churches. The effect has been to weaken our motivation and significantly reduce our impact. Steve Richardson has done an outstanding job not only of identifying the misguided thinking but also providing insightful reasoning for renewed efforts by the church to finish the task of world evangelization.

BILL JONES
Chancellor, Columbia International University; cofounder of Crossover Global

Steve has put into words what many who work in missions leadership have observed but been unable to voice. Namely, mission myths have led to a pandemic of ignorance about the realities and opportunities of mission. In a practical and winsome way, he walks the reader through the shibboleths of our day, ending with a call to join Jesus in the Greatest of Commissions.

TED ESLER
President, Missio Nexus

Thanks to Steve Richardson for this important book that not only exposes the myths about missions commonly held today but also gives key insights on the changing role of Westerners in our quest to fulfill the Great Commission. Steve is uniquely qualified to address these issues, living the life of a missionary and leading one of the largest and most innovative mission organizations in the world.

DURWOOD SNEAD
Retired Mission Pastor, North Point Mini

The debate over responsibility for the Great Commission is an enduring feature of Christian mission. The modern missionary movement was widely influenced by an important article to the churches that questioned their responsibility to go and make disciples of all nations. In that tradition, Steve Richardson offers thoughtful responses to eight common concerns about missions found in churches today. The book is ideal for small groups and church mission committees to foster a discussion of the role of individuals and churches in fulfilling God's mission for the world. Richardson's writing invites you to participate in a way that will result in significant outcomes.

Doug McConnell
Senior Professor and Provost Emeritus, School of Mission & Theology, Fuller Theological Seminary

Steve Richardson draws from decades of experience leading church-planting teams in Southeast Asia and leading an excellent international mission sending agency. He has great insights on the importance of doing missions today.

Steve Douglass
President Emeritus of Cru / Campus Crusade for Christ

Assumptions, half-truths, and sometimes even myths often influence how the church understands and engages in her God-appointed work of discipling all nations. This important book will graciously create needed tension in the heart and mind of readers so they can discern whether their Great Commission beliefs and practices are shaped by biblical convictions or by something else. I've heard it said that to do missions well, we must think about missions well. Steve's book will help you think about missions well. Read it!

Matthew Ellison
President, Sixteen:Fifteen

IS THE COMMISSION STILL GREAT?

8 MYTHS ABOUT MISSIONS &
WHAT THEY MEAN FOR THE CHURCH

STEVE RICHARDSON

MOODY PUBLISHERS

CHICAGO

All Scripture quotations, unless otherwise indicated, are taken from the Holy Bible, New International Version®, NIV®. Copyright ©1973, 1978, 1984, 2011 by Biblica, Inc.™ Used by permission of Zondervan. All rights reserved worldwide. www.zondervan.com The "NIV" and "New International Version" are trademarks registered in the United States Patent and Trademark Office by Biblica, Inc.™

Scripture quotations marked (ESV) are from the ESV® Bible (The Holy Bible, English Standard Version®), copyright © 2001 by Crossway, a publishing ministry of Good News Publishers. Used by permission. All rights reserved. The ESV text may not be quoted in any publication made available to the public by a Creative Commons license. The ESV may not be translated into any other language.

Names and details of some stories have been changed to protect the privacy of individuals.

Edited by Andrew J. Spencer
Interior design: Ragont Design
Cover design: Erik M. Peterson
Cover image of globe copyright © 2020 by Martí Sans / Stocksy (2778170). All rights reserved.
Author photo credit: Joseph Boyle

Library of Congress Cataloging-in-Publication Data

Names: Richardson, Steve (Missionary), author.
Title: Is the commission still great? : 8 myths about missions and what
  they mean for the church / Steve Richardson.
Description: Chicago : Moody Publishers, 2022. | Includes bibliographical
  references. | Summary: "Is missions an outdated idea? Do missionaries do
  harm or good? We need biblical answers to these questions. This book
  confronts the myths that threaten to undermine God's beautiful plan to
  make disciples of all nations. Christians are equipped to become joyful
  participants-not spectators-in the redemption of the world"-- Provided
  by publisher.
Identifiers: LCCN 2022021680 (print) | LCCN 2022021681 (ebook) | ISBN
  9780802429544 (paperback) | ISBN 9780802473547 (ebook)
Subjects: LCSH: Great Commission (Bible) | Missions. | BISAC: RELIGION /
  Christian Ministry / Missions | RELIGION / Christian Ministry / Pastoral
  Resources
Classification: LCC BV2074 .R53 2022 (print) | LCC BV2074 (ebook) | DDC
  266--dc23/eng/20220623
LC record available at https://lccn.loc.gov/2022021680
LC ebook record available at https://lccn.loc.gov/2022021681

Originally delivered by fleets of horse-drawn wagons, the affordable paperbacks from D. L. Moody's publishing house resourced the church and served everyday people. Now, after more than 125 years of publishing and ministry, Moody Publishers' mission remains the same—even if our delivery systems have changed a bit. For more information on other books (and resources) created from a biblical perspective, go to www.moodypublishers.com or write to:

Moody Publishers
820 N. LaSalle Boulevard
Chicago, IL 60610

1 3 5 7 9 10 8 6 4 2

Printed in the United States of America

To Arlene, my co-adventurer.
I'm so glad our fathers surmised, years ago, that we'd make
a good match. How right they turned out to be!

And to our fellow laborers in the great cause.
It's a high privilege to serve with you.

CONTENTS

WHY CARROTS AREN'T ENOUGH

In WWII Britain, night vision mattered. Cities went dark every night for six years. The blackout strategy was effective for hiding urban centers from German bombers, but it wreaked havoc on civilian life. During the first month of the war, more than a thousand people died in road accidents. While regular Britons struggled with the darkness, Royal Air Force pilots didn't seem to be having the same problem. John "Cat's Eyes" Cunningham shot down twenty Luftwaffe bombers in the dark over the course of the war, including three in a single night. Other pilots were also having remarkable success spotting enemy planes in the inky black skies. The British Air Ministry was more than happy to broadcast the secret to the RAF's nighttime prowess: their pilots ate a lot of carrots.[1]

This revelation kicked off a carrot-themed marketing campaign throughout the British Isles. The Ministry of Agriculture urged citizens to grow and eat carrots as a way to combat "blackout blindness." The Ministry of Food published recipes for everything from carrot marmalade to carrot fudge. Posters lauding the benefits of carrot consumption plastered cities. It worked too.

The British public enthusiastically embraced the humble root vegetable, which became such a staple in victory gardens that by 1942 Britain had accumulated 100,000 tons of surplus carrots.[2]

Carrot mania overflowed to the US, with the *New York Times* reporting that carrots helped the British public navigate the blackout without running into lampposts and one another. Even the Walt Disney Company got onboard with the craze, designing a family of cartoon carrots to be used in British "food propaganda." But there was a problem with the carrot craze: it was a deliberate misdirect. While carrots can help prevent night blindness caused by a vitamin A deficiency, they have no noticeable effect on a healthy person's ability to see in the dark. So why the ruse?

The promotion of carrots served two purposes for the British government, neither of which had anything to do with night vision. The practical benefit was that carrots were easy to grow and helped make up for the lack of meat, sugar, and other staples during the food shortage. The Air Ministry had a second, stealthier reason. The more people talked about carrots, the less likely they were to notice that RAF fighters had been fitted with the world's first air-to-air radar system.

German High Command may or may not have believed that the RAF pilots' alleged heavy consumption of carrots was responsible for the increase in bomber kills. Rumor has it they started feeding carrots to their pilots just in case. The connection between carrots and eyesight had enough truth to it to sound plausible, which is one reason it caught on so quickly and has endured for so long. Parents still tell their children that eating carrots will improve their eyesight.

Most misperceptions are like this: they contain at least a

kernel of truth, and they address a felt need. The British were tired of the darkness and carrots offered hope. While eating extra carrots is unlikely to cause the average person any harm, imagine if the RAF pilots had believed the propaganda. What would have become of the war effort if they had relied on carrots instead of using their new radar displays?

As followers of Jesus, we have a mission more important than any wartime strategy. We have been instructed to make disciples of every people group on earth so that a truly global church may one day worship together before the throne of God. We call that mandate the Great Commission. The magnitude of this mission is matched by its difficulty. Discipling the nations is considerably harder than shooting down bombers in the dark. Imagine explaining to people from every one of the thousands of ethnic groups in the world (after mastering the nuances of each of their languages) that two thousand years ago an infinite God provided a solution to a problem that many of them don't realize they have, and then convincing them to embrace a radical new way of life in countercultural communities under the authority of a Jewish carpenter who you insist is God incarnate. How confident do you feel about tackling that task?

The Great Commission is the most ambitious undertaking in the history of the world. It involves hundreds of millions of people and spans thousands of years. It encompasses a vast number of languages, cultures, and locations. No other endeavor—even the creation of the cosmos itself—compares with the audacity of God's redemptive plan. Adding shock to astonishment, God has entrusted a significant measure of this monumental task to weak-kneed men and women like you and me. At stake are the reputation of God and the eternal destiny of hundreds of millions of souls. Are you excited yet?

The purpose of this book is to help dispel some of the fog surrounding the nature of our mission in today's world, especially for believers in the West. Given the scale and complexity of the Great Commission, it's no wonder that misperceptions abound, even among God's people. Misunderstandings are a natural part of life, but there is more to it than that. The gospel has a very real enemy. He knows that the accomplishment of our task signals his final defeat, so he works overtime to distract, dissuade, and discourage the church. He obscures God's plan, luring us to fixate instead on lesser priorities. The enemy wants us (both individually and collectively) to trade in our core redemptive mission for a relatively innocuous existence. Let's not be distracted by carrots. God has given us radar.

1

MISSIONS IS PERIPHERAL

The goal of missions is the worship of God through the intended and eternal diversity of all people and cultures in the kingdom of God.

—F. LIONEL YOUNG, III

Perception 1: Global missions is one of many good activities. It is in the Bible but is not a central theme.

I grew up on the island of New Guinea at the junction of two rivers that fed the surrounding forests and swamps and filled them with crocodiles, cockatoos, and all manner of edible creatures and plants. Like my childhood, the Bible is framed by rivers and trees. Scripture begins in Genesis with a garden, two special trees, and a river that waters the entire region (Gen. 2:8–14). It culminates in Revelation 22 with a river "as clear as crystal" and the tree of life that brings healing to the nations (Rev. 22:1–2).

One of the most beautiful expressions of the Bible's river and tree theme is hidden in Ezekiel 47. In that passage, God shows Ezekiel a river that begins in His temple and flows deeper and stronger with time, bringing life to places of death. A small trickle from below the threshold of the temple rapidly swells in size and intensity until Ezekiel describes it as "deep enough to swim in—a river that no one could cross" (Ezek. 47:5). In the vision, Ezekiel's guide tells him that the river will turn the saltwater of the Dead Sea fresh so that "where the river flows everything will live" (Ezek. 47:9). Its banks are lined with fruitful trees "because the water from the sanctuary flows to them. Their fruit will serve for food and their leaves for healing" (Ezek. 47:12). It's an amazing picture that I believe graphically portrays God's global redemptive purposes.

In Scripture, trees and animal life are often used symbolically to represent the nations and peoples of the world. Over the ages, the Spirit of God is unfolding a plan to transform spiritual wastelands into lush gardens reverberating with the joyful worship of peoples, nations, and cultures that have been transformed by His grace. The best-known articulation of God's global intentions is found in Matthew 28:18–20, known as the Great Commission:

> Then Jesus came to [His disciples] and said, "All authority in heaven and on earth has been given to me. Therefore go and make disciples of all nations, baptizing them in the name of the Father and of the Son and of the Holy Spirit, and teaching them to obey everything I have commanded you. And surely I am with you always, to the very end of the age."

God is fulfilling the Great Commission through His people as we carry the gospel to the many communities that have yet to encounter His lavish grace. Today we call that effort, which has already been underway for two thousand years, global missions.

If God has promised to inundate the world with a torrent of life-giving spiritual water, how much time do we spend pondering the implications? Why does global missions often feel like the strange venture of a few eccentrics, something we might occasionally pray for or give money to, but otherwise consider unrelated to our daily lives? One reason may be that some of us think of the Great Commission as an idea that Jesus introduced for the first time at the end of

> **"Our church is extremely missions-minded, yet there is great apathy even here."**
>
> ~ CHURCH LEADER ~

His earthly ministry as a sort of divine afterthought: "Oh, by the way, there's something I forgot to mention . . ." But what if the Great Commission is not an afterthought at all? What if God's redemptive plan for the nations surges through the Bible like a river of life?

HOW GREAT IS THE COMMISSION?

Over the years I have frequently asked fellow believers, "What do you think are some of the misperceptions or 'myths' that keep God's people from realizing their full potential in Great Commission work?" This question provoked some stimulating exchanges, and I noticed patterns in people's responses. To confirm how common those perspectives were, I conducted an informal survey probing the prevalence of these perceptions in the North American church and their impact on our engagement with global missions. More than 120 people responded, including field missionaries, sending agency staff and board members, senior pastors, missions pastors, and missions-minded church members. You will find many of their comments highlighted throughout this book. My survey is not a source of robust statistical data, but it provides some insight into the way many missions-engaged Christians perceive the church's current understanding of missions.

When asked which of ten perceptions most hinder the North American church's missions engagement right now, 82 percent of the survey respondents (including 92 percent of church leaders) included "missions is important but not primary" in their top three choices. The idea that missions is just one of many good ways for the church to serve God had the highest survey score for impact on the church and tied for first in prevalence. More than half of the respondents said that this perception is "very much" a hindrance to missions engagement, with another third considering it as "somewhat" of a problem. Twenty-one percent rated it as "almost universal" and another 71 percent said it was "quite common." In other words, many Christians aren't sure just how great the Great Commission really is.

> "My role involves visiting a lot of church websites. In general, missions is hidden away unless you are committed to finding it."
>
> ~ MISSIONARY~

Of all the missions perceptions we will consider, the primary importance of the Great Commission is the most crucial. If we think of reaching the nations as just one of the many options God has given us for living meaningful lives that please Him, we will miss out on the most important invitation in all of history and a deep source of purpose and joy. The Great Commission is the central message of the Bible, the burning passion of God, and the primary responsibility of the church in this age.

THE THEME OF THE BIBLE

In the early years of China's reopening to the outside world, I was invited to speak to a forum of four hundred university students in Beijing. A secular political regime had deprived the Chinese people of religious input for decades. The students were smart, engaged, and hungry for new perspectives. Much to my surprise, my assigned topic was "The Theme of the Bible." How would you sum up the message of God's written revelation? What one thought ties the whole Bible together?

With little preparation besides a quick prayer, I plunged in. "Like any good book," I began, "the Bible has an introduction that sets the stage; a plotline full of colorful characters, drama, and suspense; and a spectacular conclusion with a surprise twist. *The theme of the Bible is God glorifying Himself by blessing all nations on earth through Jesus Christ, the descendant of Abraham.* God's plan for mankind began thousands of years ago and is still unfolding today. Most amazing of all, the Bible tells a real-life story in which each of us plays an important part." In other words, I told an auditorium full of secular Chinese students that the theme of the Bible is missions.

When I finished speaking, the room buzzed as the students submitted a flurry of questions scrawled in simple English and mixed in a bag to ensure their anonymity. *Where can I buy a Bible? How can I communicate with God when I can't see Him? How does someone become a Christian? Could I believe in Christianity and Buddhism at the same time?* When I presented the Bible as a unified story that makes sense of the world, the students suddenly discovered new context, beauty, and meaning for their lives. They desperately wanted to know more.

Have you ever stopped to soak in the reality that God has one worldwide, millennia-long purpose: to exalt the Lord Jesus by blessing all the nations of the earth through Him? Is it hard to believe that you have a part to play in that great cosmic drama?

The essence of the Great Commission mandate is found in all four gospels and in Acts (Matt. 28:18–20; Mark 16:15; Luke 24:46–47; John 20:21; Acts 1:8). Jesus articulated it on five different occasions, in different words, to different audiences, and with differing emphases. He had been specifically preparing His disciples for this big-picture assignment for three years, but the plan itself was much older than that. When the apostle Paul, the most influential missionary of all time, explains the biblical foundations of his calling in his New Testament writings, he doesn't mention the Great Commission as Matthew and the other gospel writers record it. Instead, in passages like Galatians 3:8 and Romans 15:8, he refers back two thousand years to the "original" Great Commission: God's covenant promise to Abraham. God's plan to redeem obedient disciples from every people group on earth had been hidden for centuries in plain sight, from Moses to Malachi. The disciples just didn't recognize it until Jesus "opened their minds so they could understand the Scriptures" after His resurrection (Luke 24:45). May He do the same for us.

Many churchgoers have a simplistic understanding of missions and only a vague sense of its importance. Others have contributed through finances and prayers for years, but nagging questions hold them back from fuller engagement. Is global missions outdated, unnecessary, or presumptuous? Is it working? And what, if anything, does it have to do with me? Church leaders, missionaries, and sending agencies have not always done a good job of providing clarity about our Great Commission roles, strategies, and progress. The good news is that God has clearly laid out His big-picture plans in Scripture.

A MESSIAH FOR ALL PEOPLES

Let's take a look at the overarching story line of the Bible with our radar engaged rather than wandering through life nibbling on carrots in hopes that they might help us see our way in the dark. In Genesis 1–11, God introduces the essential pieces of His redemption plan—creation, the fall, God's judgment in the flood, the proliferation of peoples and languages—without which the rest of the picture wouldn't make sense. In Genesis 12, God chooses Abram to initiate His two-part response to the overwhelming dilemma of sin: "I will bless you," and "all peoples on earth will be blessed through you" (Gen. 12:2–3). Paul explains in Galatians that this was a preview of the gospel and a call, ultimately, to worldwide missions. Abram responds with obedient faith, and the drama of the ages begins in earnest.

Just as Jesus gave the Great Commission five times during His ministry on earth, so the original covenant was given in its full twin-lensed format five times—three times to Abraham (Gen. 12:1–3; 18:18–19; 22:17–18), then again to Isaac (Gen. 26:3–4), and to Jacob (Gen. 28:13–15). We call these men the patriarchs because they are the first recipients of the heavenly promise and God's global mission statement. They are the ones to whom God announced the plan that would become the theme of the Bible. This promise was so important to God that even He, who cannot lie, bound Himself with an oath to fulfill it (Heb. 6:17–18). To make the scale of His intentions abundantly clear, God further promised that Abraham's descendants would be as numerous as the stars, the sand, and the dust. It's hard to imagine more comprehensive descriptors of the ultimate outcome of God's global plan.

The rest of the Old Testament unfolds against the backdrop of the Bible's redemptive theme. Abraham learns to walk by faith and become a blessing (though imperfectly) to surrounding peoples. Joseph blesses Egypt as well as his own family, with messianic foreshadowing. The Jewish people are forged as a nation during their bondage in Egypt, and their dramatic exodus reverberates to this day. Israel is called to be a "kingdom of priests," standing in the gap on behalf of the nations of the earth, illustrated through the stories of Jethro, Rahab, Ruth, and many others.

Psalm 67 explicitly describes Israel's missional role. The psalmist cries out for blessing "so that [God's] ways may be known on earth, [His] salvation among all nations" (Ps. 67:2). Echoing the Abrahamic covenant once again, Psalm 72:17 declares, "Then all nations will be blessed through him, and they will call him blessed." At least fifty other psalms feature similar statements. Remove the multicultural dimensions of the Old Testament, and very little remains.

Israel's era of God-honoring faithfulness didn't last long. She largely defaulted on her assignment to bless the nations of the world. One of the saddest verses in the Bible is Isaiah 26:18: "We were with child, we writhed in labor, but we gave birth to wind. We have not brought salvation to the earth, and the people of the world have not come to life." National disobedience resulted in destruction and exile, and yet hope still remained. Had God not bound Himself by oath? A Messiah had been promised, and

His job description was clear: "It is too small a thing for you to be my servant to restore the tribes of Jacob and bring back those of Israel I have kept. I will also make you a light for the Gentiles, that my salvation may reach to the ends of the earth" (Isa. 49:6).

In the "fullness of time," Jesus the Son of God arrived, heralded by angels, shepherds, and an international delegation bearing gifts fit for a king. His mission was to "shine on those living in darkness and in the shadow of death, to guide our feet into the path of peace" (Luke 1:79)—a reference to the Gentile (non-Jewish) world. Simeon prophesied that Jesus would be "a light for revelation to the Gentiles" (Luke 2:32).

Nazareth in Galilee of the Gentiles seemed like an improbable hometown for a Jewish messianic figure, but it fit perfectly with God's mission. Jesus came "to seek and to save the lost" (Luke 19:10), not just in Israel but all over the globe. He provided the atoning sacrifice for all who would believe, demonstrating how much "God so loved the world" (John 3:16). Jesus' death, resurrection, commissioning of the disciples, and sending of the Holy Spirit revealed the next stage of God's plan. The invitation to new birth was for everyone. You don't have to leave your culture and become a Jew to be a part of God's redemptive plan anymore. Galatians 3:29, for example, assures us that Gentiles who belong to Christ are "Abraham's seed, and heirs according to the promise."

The book of Acts documents a dramatic new phase in the redemptive strategy. Instead of the Jewish nation functioning as the primary vehicle of God's blessing, the church—a community of believing Jews and Gentiles—becomes the conduit of salvation for the nations. We are so accustomed to the idea of Gentiles enjoying equal access to God that it's hard to appreciate how radical this new arrangement was. The change from a centripetal model (come and see) to a centrifugal model (go and tell) had huge implications. Paul was God's improbable instrument to lead the nascent church into this new chapter. The transforming power of the gospel message began to permeate the Roman world from Jerusalem first and then springboarded west from Antioch. The race was on to see the "power of God that brings salvation to everyone who believes" released to the ends of the earth (Rom. 1:16). And the race is still on, just the runners are now different. Now it's our generation's turn to run.

The Bible closes with climactic scenes in the book of Revelation, giving us a preview of our final destiny. All nations will eventually worship God and His Christ (Rev. 7:9). Multitudes from the East and the West and the North and the South will sit down for a great feast with Abraham, Isaac, and Jacob, the original recipients of God's covenant promise, to celebrate the completion of global redemption.

The book of Revelation describes the end of this seminal part of history, but it's really just the beginning of the rest of eternity. The redemption of representatives from all the peoples of the earth will be a source of unending worship and celebration. Isaiah 9:7 prophesies an expansion of Christ's governance for eternal ages to come. You and I have only the tiniest comprehension—even with all that we can see from our current historical vantage point—of the scale of what God is doing. We can begin to appreciate, however, that global missions (the advance of God's kingdom through the spread of the gospel to all cultures and communities) is indeed the central theme of the Bible and the mission of His people in this age. Are you playing your part in the story of the redemption of the world? Or do you live as if the Great Commission were an afterthought?

CARROTS DOWN, EYES UP

When I go jogging, if I'm not careful, my eyes automatically focus on the ground right in front of my feet. Looking down is probably a self-protective instinct. The problem is that looking at my feet helps me avoid roots and potholes, but not tree branches or cars. It's actually not safer, though it feels that way. I can see where I am but not where I'm going or any of the splendor of the world around me. When I look down, every curb looks the same and I miss the sunrise entirely. Based on my interactions with missionaries, sending agency staff, church leaders, and missions-minded believers, I fear that we in the North American church often stare at our feet rather than fixing our eyes on the glorious redemptive mission our Lord has called us to pursue.

At a key moment in His earthly ministry, Jesus prompted His disciples to lift up their eyes and take in the big picture. Returning from a shopping excursion in the town of Sychar, the disciples were surprised to find Jesus conversing with a Samaritan woman. While the Twelve urged Him to eat, the woman ran back into the town the disciples had just left, told everyone that she had met the Messiah, and led them back to Jesus. As a result of her testimony, many people believed and were saved (John 4:39).

The disciples were caught staring, metaphorically speaking, at their own feet. They had focused on their physical needs and cultural conventions rather than sharing the message of salvation. They missed the fact that this community was ready to accept Jesus as the promised Messiah, so they missed out on an opportunity to be the initial messengers of the gospel to a receptive people. Seeing a teaching opportunity for His disciples, Jesus challenged them, "Open your eyes and look at the fields" (John 4:35).

Like Jesus' disciples, we need to periodically lift our eyes and remember the big picture. Otherwise, we may think we are on stable footing, but we won't know where we're going, and we certainly won't enjoy the view along the way. If we are not clear that God is love, and that His love extends equally to people of all nations, and if His "marching orders" are ambiguous to us, we may easily become discouraged, distracted, and apathetic.

Most of the perceptions of global missions that hinder believers from participating stem from this core problem: too many of us have lost sight of God's big-picture priority of blessing all the peoples of the world through Jesus. There is more to the Christian life than dying and going to heaven. God's methods are often mysterious, but His overall purpose is clearly laid out for us in Scripture. Let's not drift through life with good intentions but no sense of direction. Don't live as if the Great Commission is merely a suggestion.

THE SCALE OF THE MISSION

God's global mission is breathtaking in its scope. While "make disciples of all nations" may sound like simple enough instructions, we can barely even begin to grasp what is involved in such a vast and elaborate plan. The Greek word often translated "nations" in Matthew 28:19 refers to ethnolinguistic people groups, not political nations. We have identified at least ten thousand such groups, and there may be many more. Some are further subdivided by geopolitical borders or by subcultures and dialects.

For example, I grew up in a New Guinea tribe that consisted of only about three thousand people at the time but was divided into two distinct dialects. Each of the eighteen villages also had a unique accent, even though they were only separated by a few miles of jungle.

The world's people groups not only speak different languages and dialects, but they also have different worldviews. They value different things, organize ideas in different ways, and express emotions differently. Some Indonesian friends once shocked me by laughing as we drove past a terrible highway accident. Later I learned that in their culture, laughter is a common response to stress. On another occasion, an official asked for the pen in my pocket. I chuckled and turned him down because I thought it was just casual banter. To my dismay, he was deeply offended at my culturally inappropriate laughter.

Taking the gospel across cultures presents many challenges. Cultures have different ways of organizing leadership, making decisions, and viewing success. Even family structures can look very different. My sister-in-law, for example, is Minangkabau, a highly unusual people group because they are both matriarchal and Muslim (she is one of the few Christians in this people group of seven million). In every culture, values and ways of life are passed down through thousands of years of tradition and history and literature and art, some of which retain aspects of biblical truth, and some of which have been distorted by sin. Reaching so many diverse cultures with the gospel is a dizzyingly complex task.

Most of us will only come to deeply understand one or two cultures in our lifetimes. In our own culture we are like fish swimming in water, hardly aware of its influence. We know all the rules intuitively. The diversity of humanity, however, exceeds anything we can imagine. The geographical, historical, cultural, political, linguistic, and economic obstacles to the fulfillment of Jesus' Great Commission mandate are already daunting, even before we consider the spiritual dimension. So how can we possibly face such a vast, formidable task? If millions of believers over thousands of years have yet to complete the mission, who are we to attempt it?

AN ASSURED OUTCOME

The Great Commission is God's idea, not ours. Our confidence to engage in Great Commission work comes from the identity of the One who calls us and the resources He has provided. Jesus described His Father as "the Lord of the harvest" (Luke 10:2). In Matthew's text the command to make disciples is immediately preceded by the words, "All authority in heaven and on earth has been given to me," and followed by the promise, "I am with you always, to the very end of the age" (Matt. 28:18–20). God did not explain His purpose and then leave us to carry it out under our own power. He works with us and through us, empowering us by His Holy Spirit who can lift long-entrenched spiritual blinders and give "new birth" to people from Muslim, Buddhist, Hindu, animist, and secular societies. Only He can transform them (and us) into mature, obedient followers of Christ who are able to lead and disciple others.

While God's mission for the church may feel overwhelming, He has not left us without role models. The historical record is unclear on some of the details, but we know that the disciples took Jesus' command to make disciples of all nations very seriously. They spread the gospel across the known world in the first century. According to church tradition, Peter and Paul were martyred in Rome, and most of the other disciples endured violent deaths in foreign lands. Andrew preached the gospel in modern-day Turkey, Greece, and the former Soviet Union. Thomas went east to Syria with Matthias and then possibly as far as India. Bartholomew may have joined Thomas in India, then traveled through Armenia, Ethiopia, and southern Arabia. Philip preached in North Africa and Asia Minor. Matthew ministered in Ethiopia, James in Syria, Simon in Persia.[1]

The first-century church in Rome summarized Paul's life this way:

> After he had been seven times in chains, had been driven into exile, had been stoned, and had preached in the east and in the west, he won the genuine glory for his faith, having taught righteousness to the whole world and having reached the farthest limits of the west.[2]

May we all show the same courage and commitment! This does not mean that all of us need to get on airplanes and fly away to distant lands. Great Commission work is so vast and so complex that there are as many ways to engage as there are willing participants. When we understand our corporate purpose as a global church, then we are each free to pursue it wholeheartedly according to the opportunities, giftings, resources, skills, education, and experiences that God graciously gives us as individuals. Take heart—you are not responsible to "finish" the Great Commission. You are only responsible to be faithful in your small part of God's eternal plan.

Misperceptions about missions don't threaten the ultimate accomplishment of God's purposes. I have no doubt that "this gospel of the kingdom will be preached in the whole world as a testimony to all nations" (Matt. 24:14). In God's time, "the earth will be filled with the knowledge of the glory of the LORD as the waters cover the sea" (Hab. 2:14). As the Lord of the harvest, God will fulfill His promise to Abraham. He will bless all peoples through His Son. When He is finished, we will stand back in awe at what He has done, overwhelmed with gratitude that we were invited to participate in such a glorious task.

> **"Don't miss out! Be a part of reaching the last people on earth with the gospel! God will get the job done with or without you . . . so get on board while you can."**
>
> ~ MISSIONARY ~

I can imagine no greater privilege than to work alongside my Father to make known what Christ has accomplished. The key question we should each be asking ourselves is, *Am I wholeheartedly and strategically participating in His great plan?* We need clear vision to joyfully pursue God's glory among the nations. Whether we physically go to the ends of the earth as missionaries ourselves or contribute in other ways, those of us who organize our lives around the Great Commission will find deep satisfaction in this life and eternal reward in the next.

THE BOTTOM LINE

NFL lineman Jim Marshall was part of the revered "Purple People Eater" Minnesota Viking defensive line. For twenty seasons he never missed a game, earning a reputation for toughness and reliability. In 1964, playing against the San Francisco 49ers,

Marshall recovered a fumble in the fourth quarter and ran untouched for sixty-six yards to the end zone. After crossing the goal line, he tossed the ball away and began celebrating. Imagine his surprise when an opposing player trotted up, patted him on the back, and thanked him. Marshall suddenly realized that he was standing in the wrong end zone.[3] He had just scored a safety, giving two points to the 49ers.[4] In football, as in much of life, it doesn't matter that you're doing something earnestly if you aren't doing the right thing.

My daughter Kelly had a similar experience to Jim Marshall at one of her kindergarten sports days. During a race with her classmates, she became disoriented and ran in the wrong direction. My wife and I, along with everyone else, shouted to her to turn around and go the other way. Kelly thought we were cheering her on, so she ran even faster. She was motivated and diligent. She just wasn't running in the right direction.

Running the wrong way in kindergarten is an adorable mishap. In the NFL, it's a big deal. In the Christian life, neglecting our Great Commission purpose can be an eternal loss, both for us and for the worldwide church. God has sovereignly chosen to make His church the conduit of His blessing to all the peoples of the world. He commands all believers to participate in His great campaign of mercy and love and has entrusted the gospel to us. In the final analysis, when God reviews our lives, it won't just be about our sincerity or discipline. It'll be about whether we did what He instructed us to do. Did we give ourselves wholeheartedly to the mission? Did we run hard in the right direction?

Even if we start off running in the right direction, we need continuing reminders and markers to stay the course. Mission drift is a real threat, both for individuals and organizations. For example, Harvard University was founded in 1636 with the motto, "Truth for Christ and the Church." The original mission statement reads: "Let every student be plainly instructed and earnestly pressed to consider well the end of his life and studies is to know God and Jesus Christ, which is eternal life, and therefore to lay Christ in the bottom, as the only foundation of all sound knowledge and learning."[5] Eighty years later, a group of pastors established a new school to be a stronghold of Christian higher education because they were concerned that Harvard had drifted too far from its original mission. They called it Yale. The cycle repeated. Neither school has a reputation for theological conviction or Christian character today.[6] If mission drift happens to large institutions started by Christians, aren't individual believers and congregations also in danger of losing sight of their primary mission over time?

> "God purposefully designed each follower to assist Him in the work He is doing around the world. He wants to show you the greater purpose He has for you."
>
> ~ MISSIONARY~

No one likes to think that their ideas are faulty or incomplete, but correcting misinformation can actually be a positive, motivating experience. I believe that a proper understanding of global missions will remind us of the immense privilege we have of aligning our lives with God's will. My prayer is that the process of reflection and learning will give us a clearer picture of what God is calling us to do and inspire us with the glory of His big-picture plan for the world.

Don't let the enemy distract you from your purpose, convince you that it is only for other people, or discourage you that it can't be done. If we miss the big picture, staring myopically at our feet as we run in the wrong direction, we may feel that we are being safety conscious, but we will miss out on the purpose for which our Lord created us. Lift up your eyes to the harvest. When we and our local churches organize our lives around the Great Commission mandate, then everything else will fall into alignment. May God's global redemptive purpose take its proper place as the central theme not just of the Bible, but of our lives and our churches as well.

WHAT'S COMING NEXT

In the next chapters we will unpack seven more common perceptions of missions and missionaries that can distract or discourage the people of God from fully engaging in the Great Commission. You may share some of these views yourself, or you may hear them from other people. For example, shouldn't the lost hear the gospel from Christians in their own countries rather than from foreign missionaries? Isn't it better to send lots of people on short trips than a few people for a lifetime? Could missions be doing more harm than good? Each perception we will consider has at least a kernel of truth to it. However, if our understanding of these topics is inaccurate, incomplete, or imbalanced, the church can quickly become apathetic or skeptical about fully engaging in global missions.

By design, this book provides only a brief treatment of each subject. Not everyone will agree with me on every point, and that's okay. The Great Commission is not only a global task, but also a communal one. God has equipped the church with an abundance of resources and a robust immune system so that we can refine our understanding of our global mandate together.

I hope this material stimulates conversations in local churches. At the conclusion of each chapter, I have included discussion questions to help church members dive deeper into God's magnificent plan to redeem all the peoples of the world.

DISCUSSION QUESTIONS

1. Do you agree that God wants to glorify Himself by blessing all the nations on earth through Jesus Christ, the descendant of Abraham? Do you see that as the theme of the Bible?

2. What distracts you from that big-picture plan or discourages you from getting more involved?

3. What activities or resources help you lift your eyes to the harvest and take in God's big-picture plan for the world?

2

WESTERN MISSIONARIES ARE OBSOLETE

*The burden of proof rests upon you to show that the circumstances
in which God has placed you were meant
by Him to keep you out of the foreign mission field.*

—ION KEITH-FALCONER

Perception 2: Western missionaries are not needed as they
once were. The church is growing in other parts of the world,
and local Christians can do a better job of reaching their own
people.

During the period when the iPod was competing with Microsoft's Zune for market share, author Simon Sinek was invited to
speak at Apple. He tells the story of trying to provoke a debate
with an Apple executive by commenting that the Zune was a
better device. The executive simply replied, "I have no doubt,"
and moved on to another subject. Sinek was surprised that such
a senior leader wouldn't defend his product. He was even more
surprised, along with the rest of the world, when Apple launched

the iPhone a year later, changing the way we interact with technology and making both the iPod and the Zune irrelevant.[1]

HAVE WESTERN MISSIONARIES GONE THE WAY OF THE ZUNE?

Within the North American church there is a growing sentiment that sending career cross-cultural missionaries from the West is anachronistic. We still enjoy the occasional inspiring story of a missionary hero like Hudson Taylor or Elisabeth Elliot to add drama to a Sunday sermon, but we think of such people as largely belonging to a bygone era. Missions conferences, once an important annual event for many churches, are increasingly becoming a relic of the past. In many contexts, a long-term Western missionary elicits the same reaction as a typewriter in an antique shop: "We used to have one of those!"

When asked which perceptions of missions most hindered believers' engagement in Great Commission work, about a quarter of our survey respondents included "missionaries are obsolete" in their top three rankings. Well over half said that this perception is "quite common" or "almost universal" in the North American church, and more than two-thirds said that it impacts missions participation "somewhat" or "very much." If our survey respondents are correct, many of God's people in North America believe that missionary sending can—or even should—now be delegated to Christians in other parts of the world. Many believers are therefore less motivated to actively participate in sending long-term missionaries from their own churches.

WHAT'S BEHIND THE PERCEPTION?

For some Christians, the assumption that missions is no longer relevant, or at least that Western missionaries no longer need to be sent, is simply a lack of awareness. Missions is not part of their everyday lives, and so they don't give it much thought. Just as someone can attend church for years without actually hearing and responding to the gospel, some faithful church members are never confronted with the reality of a lost world and God's plan for reaching it.

> "I think there is a growing sense that 1) the gospel has already gone everywhere, 2) nationals can do it better and cheaper, and 3) strategic use of resources by the American church is almost exclusively a financial matter."
>
> ~ MISSIONARY~

Other believers, however, thoughtfully consider the issue and conclude that the era of Western missionary sending is drawing to a close. The pace of change in the world, including the missions world, has accelerated dramatically in recent decades. Any significant change requires recalibration, and sometimes the disruption is severe enough to demand all-out reinvention. Global missions is not exempt from that type of disruption. We must evaluate our roles, methodologies, and training, taking present realities and trends into account. Let's identify some of the questions that cause believers to wonder whether Western missionaries are obsolete. Then we'll consider the situation again in light of God's big-picture redemption plan.

1. Isn't the church growing worldwide?

Indeed, it is! The growth and redistribution of the church in the last century is nothing short of astonishing. Consider a few representative statistics:

> In 1900, 82 percent of Christians lived in Europe and North America. In 2020, that figure dropped to 33 percent.

> In 2014, Latin America surpassed Europe as the continent with the most Christians. In 2018, Africa overtook Latin America.

> More Christians speak Spanish than English as their mother tongue.[2]

> In 2020, of the ten countries with the most evangelicals, nine were in the Global South.[3]

To distinguish between areas where the church has long been established and places where it has begun to grow more recently, we commonly use the terms "West" and "Global South." The Global South includes countries with developing economies in Latin America, Africa, Asia, and Oceania. In traditional missions parlance, these countries have historically been described as "receiving" regions. "Global South" is not a geographically precise term, as Australia and New Zealand are considered Western countries even though they are in the South, and China is part of the Global South even though it is located well above the equator. The distinctions between the West and the Global South are growing less clear as economic and other differences diminish in a globalizing world. When discussing the expansion of the church, however, these labels are still helpful and widely used.

The *World Christian Encyclopedia* summarizes the current makeup of the body of Christ this way:

> The number of Evangelicals in the world has increased from 112 million in 1970 to 386 million in 2020. Globally, Evangelicalism is a predominantly non-White movement within Christianity, and becoming increasingly more so, with 77% of all Evangelicals living in the Global South in 2020. This is up from only 7.8% in 1900. This reality runs against the popular perception in the West that the United States is the "home" of contemporary Evangelicalism, where Evangelicalism is a largely White, politically conservative movement.[4]

Clearly the missions landscape has changed. Gina Zurlo points out, "A typical Christian today is a non-white woman living in the global South, with lower-than-average levels of societal safety and proper health care. This represents a vastly different typical Christian than that of 100 years ago, who was likely a white, affluent European."[5] In *The New Shape of World Christianity*, Mark Noll writes, "The Christian church has experienced a larger geographical redistribution in the last fifty years than in any comparable period in its history, with the exception of the very earliest years of church history."[6]

Western Christians can take great encouragement in the vast and growing number of believers across Asia, Africa, Oceania, and Latin America. God is being worshiped in thousands of languages and honored in thousands of cultures. Does this dramatic new growth mean that the church of the Global South is ready to take the missions baton from the church in the West?

2. Isn't globalization already giving everyone access to the gospel?

I found myself relaxing one evening as a guest in the home of a prominent Muslim family in Afghanistan. Family members scurried about making final preparations for a feast. One of the few reminders that I hadn't been transported into biblical times was a prominent TV, its volume uncomfortably high despite the many conversations swirling around the bustling living room. The broadcast eventually transitioned to a new show and the people around me suddenly stopped talking and zeroed in on the screen.

As I watched, the show's host produced a book, which I recognized as a Bible. He began explaining in Farsi how to read the book and learn from it. He went on to demonstrate how it can be helpful to read the Bible in a small group or as a family, and how to ask questions that enhance the group learning process. I was impressed not only by the reach and effectiveness of the satellite broadcast, but also by the rapt attention it received from my hosts. What a privilege to witness the gospel arriving, perhaps for the first time, in the home of this Afghan family!

The opportunities for gospel advancement furnished by such trends as urbanization, migration, advances in digital media, and other aspects of globalization are breathtaking. The coronavirus pandemic only accelerated the interconnectedness of the global church and the development of digital tools for evangelism and discipleship. We can now broadcast the gospel and discipleship materials into hard-to-access places all across the globe through digital media. These tools are helping the church grow in places where it is difficult to send Western missionaries. Do we still need missionaries if we have such effective tools?

3. Isn't the global church catching a vision for missions?

One of the unfortunate patterns of missions history is that, in many cases, missionaries planted churches without instilling missionary DNA. Westerners often saw themselves as an exclusive mission force reaching the rest of the world. While there are marvelous historical exceptions, missionaries often thought, "It's going to be ages before these people are ready to be missionaries themselves," and so they planted churches to be a witness in their own communities, but not necessarily beyond.

Today, equipping new churches in their own sending vision and capacity is an increasingly significant role for Western missionaries. Many national churches are catching their own vision for the Great Commission. This opens the door to cross-cultural *multiplication*, not just internal *addition*. One church in Brazil, for example, is committed to sending out four hundred missionaries. An indigenous African mission organization has seven hundred workers serving in thirty-six countries.

Missions is no longer primarily the work of Westerners bringing the gospel to everyone else. In 1974, missionaries from the Global South numbered around six thousand. By the year 2000, there were sixty thousand. In 2010, more than three hundred thousand non-Western missionaries were engaged in reaching the world.[7] *Operation World* reminds us, "When praying for those many places in the world that need more missionaries, pray with an awareness that the answer may come from east, west, north or south, from a neighbouring culture or one on the other side of the world."[8] The church of the Global South is ready and willing to take up the worldwide cause of the Great Commission. If there are so many of them, do they still need us?

4. Aren't Global South missionaries more effective?

Absolutely, sometimes they are. Consider the example of Setia, an on-fire believer who lives in a town surrounded by completely unreached people groups. She has an IT degree but focuses almost entirely on reaching the lost and lifting people out of poverty, and she shares her faith constantly as she does so.

> "The rising tide is, 'Let's pay the church of the Global South to do it.'"
>
> ~ MISSIONARY ~

Setia started a recycling center to help people who were surviving off the local garbage dump. City officials watched drug addicts and alcoholics transform into productive members of society and were so impressed that they gave Setia a facility to use. The country's president even visited and highlighted her recycling center on national television as an example of selfless citizenship!

My wife and I had the privilege of meeting Setia early on in her ministry. Arlene connects with her daily, mentoring and encouraging her through text messages. Sometimes we wonder who is really mentoring whom! They share prayer requests in real time. Each month we send her a modest amount of financial support to help sustain her life and ministry. It's as if she's the apostle Paul and we are the church in Philippi.

Setia has opened a shop to sell handicrafts made by people she reached with the gospel. She hosts Bible studies in the back room. When Muslims come to faith, she baptizes them in the ocean. Discipling young converts from Islam is a natural part of her lifestyle. Setia is more comfortable in the local culture than most Westerners ever become, and she evangelizes and disciples without any of the awkwardness or Western baggage that foreign missionaries inevitably bring. She's flexible and prepared for virtually any opportunity that comes her way.

Setia isn't the only local evangelist that my wife and I support who has no formal connection to a Western mission agency. These are people with whom we've built personal relationships over the years. They are on-site, helping to reach unreached people groups. It feels like a modern-day book of Acts—a beautiful picture of the body of Christ at work. We live in remarkable times. If people like Setia are available and fruitful, where does that leave the rest of us? Do we still have a role aside from providing financial support?

5. Aren't non-Western missionaries much cheaper?

"Does Pioneers have a retirement plan for its missionaries?" This was one of the first questions a church missions committee asked when Arlene and I first interviewed for support years ago. They wisely wanted to avoid being saddled with us in our old age, distant as that may have seemed at the time. It was a reminder how different our world is from that of an average believer in Peru or Tanzania. While many economies have improved noticeably over the last few decades, the cost-of-living differential is still great. Many people in the Global South live on a few hundred dollars a month, at the most, not a few thousand as we generally do in the West.

Most Western missionaries receive rather modest salaries by their own culture's standards, but by the time you add insurance, travel, retirement, ministry projects, visas, children's schooling, and overhead, the cost can easily reach $75,000 a year for a family of four. How can we justify the cost of sending one Western family when we could support a dozen evangelists from the Global South for the same amount of money?

6. Isn't my home city and country becoming a mission field too?

Christianity does indeed appear to be regressing in certain parts of the world that we once considered reached. Gordon Olson writes, "Europe has gone from being a 'Christian continent' to becoming a secularized continent in need of evangelization again."[9] Seventeen European countries are less than 1 percent evangelical.[10] Less than 10 percent of French people own Bibles and only 20 percent have ever interacted with one.[11] Many would say the same of the US, where the number of people who identify themselves as non-religious has grown from 6 percent to 23 percent in the last thirty years.[12] *Operation World* sums it up: "The religious canvas of American life is being repainted before our eyes."[13]

In addition to the need for re-evangelizing nations that we have historically thought of as Christian, the West has become home to people from the neediest and least-reached places in the world. The UN estimates that in 2019, 272 million people lived outside their birth countries.[14] That's about one in thirty people on earth. Eighty-two million of these international migrants live in Europe, with another fifty-nine million settling in North America. New York City is currently home to speakers of some 800 languages.[15] Even ten years ago, nearly half of Toronto's residents spoke one of two hundred mother tongues besides French or English.[16] Clearly, there is much work to do in our own backyard. If the world is coming to us, why would we send missionaries away to distant lands?

DOES THIS MEAN THAT
WESTERN WORKERS AREN'T NEEDED?

We've seen that the center of gravity of the worldwide church has shifted definitively toward the Global South. Western missionaries are expensive and there is much to do in our homelands. Global South churches are sending out their own members as effective cross-cultural workers. Do all these developments imply that Western missionaries are becoming obsolete? Does the growing presence of faithful believers like our friend Setia mean that we can stop sending missionaries? Does the dramatic shift in Christian demographics mean that the historical missionary-sending powerhouses of the past (the church in North America and in Europe) are the Zunes and iPods of redemptive history?

Some well-meaning, thoughtful believers have concluded that we are wasting time and money investing in Western missionaries who are rapidly being made irrelevant by the globalization of the church. They argue that we have been so successful in discipling other parts of the world that they no longer need us to participate beyond sending money. No one wants to be Microsoft clinging to their Zune while Apple changes the world. For me, all this good news about the church in the Global South has the opposite effect. It makes me want to mobilize even more workers for the ripening harvest. And I want to see them coming from everywhere.

There's a reason we call the Great Commission a "commission." It's an authoritative command—a call to action. Just as

God sent His Son, so Jesus sends us. John's gospel uses two different words to describe Jesus' mission. *Apostello* emphasizes the role of someone sent on a mission with unquestionable authority. *Pempo* has more to do with the act of sending. Jesus combines the two for emphasis in John 20:21, "As the Father has sent [*apostello*] me, I am sending [*pempo*] you."

Between Jesus' resurrection and His ascension, He hammered home one central message for His disciples: they had a mission to make disciples everywhere in the world, and the Holy Spirit would soon be sent specifically to empower them for that task. All five distinct conversations in which Jesus gave His disciples their Great Commission marching orders involved a call to movement and to global action. Grammatically, "make disciples" is the primary verb of Matthew 28:19, but that doesn't mean that *going* is a dispensable or negotiable part of the process.

For centuries, the Lord's Prayer has been recited in churches: "Our Father, who art in heaven . . ." The other prayer that Jesus instructed His disciples to pray gets repeated far less often: "Ask the Lord of the harvest, therefore, to *send out* workers into his harvest field" (Matt. 9:38, emphasis added). The word for "send" here is *ekballo*, which implies a forceful thrusting out, a "throwing" or "compelling." It's the same term used for casting out a demon. The Lord of the harvest literally compels His workforce to go out into all parts of the harvest. There is a tremendous sense of urgency.

Now, am I suggesting that every Christian must physically relocate to another country? Of course not. Am I saying that going and making disciples doesn't include using media, praying fervently, nurturing our families, furthering the sanctification of believers wherever they are, and multiplying churches in our own neighborhoods and cities? Not at all. We need to do all those things. What I'm suggesting is that any ministry paradigm that doesn't include the equipping and sending of qualified workers into the least-reached cultures of the world is incomplete. Going is not optional, even for Westerners. Let's consider some counterpoints to the questions we asked in the last section of this chapter. Ending "flesh and blood" involvement in the Great Commission may not be such a great idea after all.

1. The church in the Global South is growing, and they want to partner with us, not replace us.

In my travels I sometimes have the opportunity to ask local church leaders, "Do you still want missionaries from the West?" They almost always answer, "Yes"—with caveats. "We want you to send us the right kind of people, with a humble posture, who are willing to serve alongside us and model Christlikeness." As in any massive and complex undertaking, everyone makes mistakes, and everyone has their horror stories. Churches around the world have sometimes wearied of Western workers who don't last long or who come with grand but short-lived plans and strategies. Nonetheless, I've encountered a desire in the Global South for the right kinds of people bringing the right kinds of help. Should we not respond?

> "There are many, many places that need Christian missionaries from any country. I don't see why Americans should be excluded if they answer the call."
>
> ~ CHURCH LEADER ~

God has given the Western church a marvelous stewardship responsibility by blessing us with immense financial resources. Our history—of missionary sending, missiological learning, organizational development, strategic thinking, disciplined giving patterns, and creative mobilization approaches—is a gold mine of information and experience for the global church. Not infrequently, delegations of students, seminarians, and church leaders from around the world visit our Pioneers office in Orlando seeking insights that will enrich their own mission efforts. They want to serve together with us, not replace us. And that includes partnering with Western workers who go, just as they themselves are sending more and more of their own members. This is no time to quit.

2. Technology provides wider access to the gospel, but the needs are still vast.

Sometimes it's hard to hold good news and bad news in tension. We like to focus on one or the other. The scale of the Great Commission is so great that both realities apply: tremendous progress is being made, and we're still far from done. Flying from Southeast Asia to Europe one night, I gazed down for a couple of hours on the glimmering lights of India's towns and cities, representing a population soon to surpass that of China. Of the nearly 1.4 billion precious people whose lights I saw that night, hundreds of millions still have little if any understanding of the gospel. I found it too much to take in. When I travel in Europe and Latin America, that sense of an overwhelming need and challenge is the same. The harvest is ripe, and the laborers are so few. That's how Jesus saw the world, and it's still true today.

Vast numbers of people have still never heard the message of salvation. Hundreds of millions of people live in places where there is no church. They probably don't know a Christian and couldn't find a Bible in their language if they wanted one.

And even if there is a church nearby, they still don't necessarily have access to the gospel. The presence of a church in a city, for example, does not mean that every people group who lives in that city can now hear the gospel. Cultural and language barriers are not tied to geography. In some places, believers from reached peoples worship in churches only a few blocks from communities of unengaged peoples. A group is usually defined as *unengaged* if it has no known church planting effort underway. Believers may live nearby but speak a language that their unreached neighbors do not understand. They might use religious forms that are appropriate in their own culture, but confusing or offensive to others.

> "Some church members have switched their missions giving to 'local believers' because they think it is more effective. When we explain that there are no local believers in many places, it seems to be a surprise to them."
>
> ~ MISSIONARY ~

The thought of the global church working together to engage all the unreached people groups in the world with the gospel in the next decade is thrilling. But engaging every people group is not yet the fulfillment of the Great Commission. It is, to borrow Winston Churchill's wisdom, only "the end of the beginning."[17] The Great Commission is to make disciples of every people group, baptize them, and teach them to obey everything Jesus commanded. That will likely take us quite some time.

You may wonder, *Can't the churches that missionaries planted finish what they started?* And the answer is that yes, sometimes they can. Church movements do carry on within many cultures, building on the initial foundation and momentum of pioneer missionary work. At a certain point, foreign missionaries may be unnecessary or even detrimental to the development of the local church. However, movements seldom cross language and cultural boundaries without intentional missionary effort. Natural church multiplication tends to happen within people groups. Crossing political, cultural, and linguistic boundaries requires special focus and skills. As a result, while "the church is bigger than you think" (to borrow an old book title), thousands of people groups still have almost no one who can disciple them in a culturally relevant way. Tens of thousands of missionaries are still needed to catalyze that cross-cultural process. I believe that some of those missionaries can and should come from the West.

> "The push for locally led ministry is needed and wonderful, but sometimes locals have a hard time if not harder time ministering where Westerners can more easily because of biases, racism, and historical prejudice."
>
> ~ MISSIONARY ~

3. The church of the Global South is catching a missions vision, but that doesn't mean we should forfeit ours.

Think for a moment about how you would feel if God informed you that He no longer wanted your church to send missionaries to other countries. How would you feel about being excluded from the greatest rescue mission in the history of the universe? Would it be a relief? The thought ought to fill us with grief, and perhaps even righteous jealousy.

Our calling is not drudgery. It's not a chore to get over with so that we can go do something more interesting and enjoyable. Discipling the nations is God's agenda for this age, the natural outworking of Christ's victory on the cross. It's the biggest, boldest, and most God-glorifying undertaking of all time, through which the "manifold wisdom of God" is being "made known to the rulers and authorities in the heavenly realms" (Eph. 3:10). It is the overarching story line of the Bible and our assignment for the short time we have on earth. Why would we prefer to be sidelined while others carry on? That would be like turning down a generous family inheritance just because our siblings are available to take over our share of the estate. It makes no sense.

4. Missionaries from the Global South are effective in ministry, but that doesn't mean Westerners aren't.

If you think about it, the presupposition behind the idea that missionaries don't need to be sent anymore is that missionaries have been successful. They've worked themselves out of a job! The Global South church that we celebrate today was built through the work of missionaries, and many of them were Westerners. Backing up a few more steps, every single Christian in the world is the result of a successful missionary endeavor at some point along the way. Every one of us owes our spiritual lives to missions.

Take the example of Setia, the highly effective missionary in an unreached area of her own country that I mentioned earlier. How did Setia become a believer? Through Western missionaries who moved to her city years ago, learned her language, and explained the gospel in a way she could understand. How can she lead evangelistic Bible studies and show the *Jesus* film? Global missions efforts produced training materials and translated the Scriptures into the languages of the people groups she is reaching.

The increasingly fruitful participation of one part of the body of Christ builds on, but doesn't negate, the ongoing responsibility of other family members. If missionaries have been successful and every one of us traces our spiritual lineage to them, why stop sending them? As my father-in-law, the founder of Pioneers, used to say, "Go with what got you there."

5. Global South missionaries are cheaper to send, but frugality is not our primary goal.

No question about it, reaching the world with the gospel comes with a cost, financial and otherwise. A lot of communication about missions involves the need for funding. We may have the impression, then, that the primary need on the field is money, and therefore we should engage the cheapest possible missionaries. My experience has been that the greatest need on the field is for Christian workers with character and grit, but I won't deny that money is an important part of the equation. So how much "bang" are we getting for our "buck"? Granted, not many people state it quite so bluntly (it sounds rather mercenary), but that's the thought that crosses many of our minds as we consider the myriad financial needs around us. It's a question of return on investment. We want to make the biggest possible difference with the resources we have to contribute.

For a time, I was part of a house church of about five families. We didn't have a church mortgage or staff salaries to cover, so we focused our giving on covering the cost of sending a family with three children to Asia as missionaries. Our ratio of senders to goers was highly unusual. Even the average North American church, however, could probably do more than they are. In 2019, evangelical Christians made up about 25 percent of the US adult population, which correlates to about eighty-three million people today.[18] If every two hundred American Christians worked together to send out one additional missionary, we would gain 415,000 more workers for the global harvest.

Dr. Ralph Winter, who popularized the idea of unreached people groups in the 1970s and founded the US Center for World Mission (now Frontier Ventures), advocated a "wartime" lifestyle, which is not identical to a "simple" lifestyle. "If a man is out in a trench and he's eating K rations, he's not using up much money," Dr. Winter explained, "but a guy who's flying a fighter plane may be using up $40,000 a month of technology. In other words, during wartime one doesn't judge according to the same model of lifestyle. What's important is getting the job done."[19] The serious pursuit of any significant endeavor, including the Great Commission, will be expensive. My point isn't to defend wasteful spending, but rather to suggest that costs and risks need to be weighed relative to the importance of the mission.

While we all seek optimal stewardship, I would caution against an overemphasis on efficiency that unduly supersedes other values, such as ensuring the involvement of a broad cross section of the body of Christ. Conversations around efficiency can be driven by the perceived limited resources. It's a necessary discussion, but let's not forget that God is ultimately the one supplying the finances and manpower for the fulfillment of the Great Commission. Efficiency is one of many factors to consider.

According to a 2022 report, the personal income of Christians worldwide is about $53 trillion, and we spent $52 billion of that on global foreign missions.[20] $52 billion dollars sounds like a lot of money, but it's only about 0.1 percent of our income. And remember, not all of that went to ministry among the unreached. Our definition of "global foreign missions" can be pretty broad. As a point of reference, the World Christian Database estimates that in 2022 more money was embezzled from Christian organizations ($59 billion) than was spent on global missions ($52 billion).[21] The church isn't short of missionaries because the ones we send are too expensive. We're short of missionaries because we haven't given missions its proper priority in our decision-making and finances.

Supporting workers from the Global South to minister in their own or nearby countries can be a strategic and cost-effective way to advance the work. So can sending Westerners to serve with humility in important cross-cultural roles. I want to see more of both. We have a responsibility to steward our resources well. We also have a direct command from the Lord Jesus to accomplish the task He gave us. If we stop sending our own people from our local churches, we will become disconnected from the work, and I predict that within one generation, we won't be sending money either.

6. There are needs in our backyard, but we must maintain an outward vision.

Behind the notion of a missionary-sending moratorium lies a risky assumption. We assume that a local church can stay healthy without sending emissaries to other communities and cultures. But what if a prime indicator of a healthy church is its outward orientation, most clearly expressed when it sends its own members into cross-cultural ministry? What if sending missionaries is not only an indicator of, but also a *prime contributor* to, the health of a church? Take note that the spiritually vibrant parts of some declining mainline denominations are found in the Global South, where churches are enthusiastically embracing the Great Commission. One of their goals is to re-evangelize the declining mother churches that birthed them. We must take care that we do not fall for an illusion of self-preservation that actually stunts and deprives our churches.

Thanks to the apostle Paul and other first-century apostolic church planters, the early church thrived and multiplied amid great opposition. As the centuries passed, the church largely lost its missionary momentum. The focus turned inward, disregarding the "uttermost parts." In time, unevangelized nations conquered North Africa and other previously Christianized lands.

To see the effect, travel through Turkey, a country of eighty-four million people, which has fewer than ten thousand known believers today. Or tour the ruins of Carthage, the home of Tertullian and the place where the New Testament canon was first formally recognized. It was later overrun by gospel-less Vandals and Umayyads. Wherever Great Commission obedience falters, the church's vibrancy begins to wane. Gospel-privileged peoples who do not keep the message flowing outward will eventually lose it themselves.

> "Some churches state outright that they are only called to reach their local area and have no need to be involved in global missions. Their reasoning: 'If the nations need to be reached, God will bring those people into our area so we can reach them here.'"
>
> ~ MISSIONARY ~

Churches that have lost their passion for global missions have at least one thing in common: they've stopped sending their own flesh and blood. It's one thing to participate in missions from a distance. It's quite another to be "in the trenches" with fellow believers in another culture, suffering, dreaming, and strategizing together about herculean challenges and spiritual attacks. This applies not only on the field side of our missions efforts but also on the sending side. Radical obedience and participation in the Great Commission is as much caught as it is taught. Virtually every candidate who applies for service with Pioneers has been significantly influenced by cross-cultural missionaries they know personally. Missions is a blessing not only to the receiving community, but also to the sending church.

THE BOTTOM LINE

Are Western missionaries obsolete? The encouraging growth of the church in the Global South is unquestionably reshaping the missions landscape. Our role and contributions are shifting. But to conclude that any segment of the church no longer has a direct role to play is a misapplication of a wonderful reality. Our Lord commanded us to pray for more laborers in the harvest, and He is answering our prayers by raising up godly and skilled emissaries from every corner of the earth. The challenge for the Western church is to redouble our efforts in fresh and creative ways.

Don't fall for the lie that Westerners are no longer needed or wanted. That is the enemy trying to invalidate our missionary heritage and deprive us of life-giving, faith-building participation in global missions. Western believers don't have to fade into obsolescence like a Zune with an out-of-date operating system. The church is a living organism made up of hundreds of millions of living people, not a product line. We can grow, adapt, improvise, learn, and innovate together. The Great Commission is for all of God's people everywhere. Jesus didn't tell us to make enough disciples so that they can finish reaching the rest of the world without us. None of us is finished until the job is done or the Lord calls us home.

DISCUSSION QUESTIONS

1. Were you surprised by the statistics about the growth of the church in the Global South?

2. Suppose someone told you that your church couldn't send missionaries anymore. How would you feel? Would you be disappointed? Relieved?

3. How do you feel about the idea of you personally, or missionaries you support, working in partnership with, and even under the leadership of, believers from the Global South?

3

EVERYTHING WE DO IS MISSIONS

*If every Christian is already considered a missionary . . . nobody
needs to get up and go anywhere to preach the gospel.
But if our only concern is to witness where we are, how will
people in unevangelized areas ever hear the gospel?*

—C. GORDON OLSON

Perception 3: All good work done in the name of Christ, especially if it involves some form of outreach, is part of missions. Every believer is a missionary in his or her setting.

We have identified the theme of the Bible as God glorifying Himself by blessing all peoples on earth through Jesus Christ, the descendant of Abraham. Scripture explains that God's people are to make disciples among all the nations under His authority and by His Spirit's enablement. If the Great Commission is a universal mandate, what does that mean for individual churches and Christians? Is everything the church does missions? Is every Christian a missionary?

In Medan, the largest city on the island of Sumatra, children start driving motorbikes before they can touch the ground and see over the handlebars at the same time. Every one of those motorbikes is referred to as a *honda*. Now, many of them are indeed Honda brand motorcycles, but a good portion are Yamahas, Suzukis, and Kawasakis. That leads to exchanges like this one, which ring a little strange to Western ears:

"Do you have a *honda*?"

"Yes. It's a Yamaha."

I suspect that neither Honda nor Yamaha marketing executives are very pleased about this phenomenon. You might think that the more a brand name is known and used, the better, but that's not always the case. We now commonly use names like Kleenex, Jacuzzi, and Frisbee—which technically designate specific brands—to refer broadly to their most popular products. Such generalization of brand names is a serious problem for companies whose products dominate the market. If their product name enters mainstream vocabulary as an item rather than a brand, they can legally lose their trademark rights. It's called *genericide*.[1]

The words "missions" and "missionary" are in danger of genericide. When my parents first went to the field, missionaries were ministers of the gospel in a long-term, full-time, cross-cultural capacity, usually overseas. During my lifetime, Christians have started using the terms "missions" and "missionaries" in a less specific way. Some Christians now define missions broadly enough to include virtually any activity of the church, including ministering within local congregations, serving the poor, and fighting injustice. Many North American churches have signs in their parking lots announcing, "You are now entering the mission field," implying that anything happening off church property qualifies as missions.

A coworker told me about a missions class in which the

teacher presented a list of Christian activities and asked people to raise their hands if they considered each one to be missions. The early examples involved cross-cultural ministry among unreached peoples, and everyone raised their hands. Further down he listed ministries closer to home, and some dropped out. The last option was, "I take soup to my Christian next-door neighbor." A few students still raised their hands to indicate that this was also missions. The teacher improvised, "What if I'm having devotions in my room by myself?" One man in the class responded, "It depends. You might be reading the book of Acts." No one denies that taking soup to a believing neighbor is kind, but does this fit within the scope of discipling the *ethne*, the peoples of the earth? Is being involved in missions really as simple as reading the book of Acts?

> **"We were invited to speak at an association of churches' missions event. Most of the time was spent talking about disaster relief in the US. We felt out of place as we talked about church planting in an unreached country."**
>
> ~ MISSIONARY ~

Defining missions is complicated because language is not static and word usage evolves over time. Some churches now talk about being *on mission* or *missional* or use the term *mission* rather than *missions*. Does the vocabulary matter? I think it depends. If a word is archaic and no longer communicates the intended meaning, then it's not worth preserving strictly for the sake of tradition. New translations of Scripture, for example, can help clarify the original meaning in more contemporary language.

According to one legend, the first Spanish explorers arriving on the coast of Central America asked the local Maya people, "What is this place called?" The natives responded, "*Yucatan!*

Yucatan!" So, the Spaniards decided to call the area the Yucatan Peninsula. Not until much later did they discover that what the foreigners had heard as *Yucatan* was actually a local phrase that meant, "We don't understand you! You're not making any sense!"[2] But the name still stuck.

Let's not stubbornly hang on to words that don't communicate important ideas, but let's also not deprive important concepts of clear labels. My concern is not that we might use different words than previous generations to talk about missions, but rather how the broadening of our missions terminology impacts our understanding of the Great Commission and our sense of responsibility to participate constructively in that task. The relevant question is not whether we are allowed to change the words. Instead, we should be asking ourselves, *Does broadening the term "missions" to include a wide range of Christian activities lead to increased engagement in the task of taking the gospel to every people group on earth?* Does calling every Christian a missionary motivate us to pursue the Great Commission more diligently? Or does it dilute our focus and distract us from the core task God has given us? As language evolves, sometimes it's worth fighting to preserve an ancient concept.

THE BROAD STROKES

When asked about perceptions that hinder the North American church's engagement with missions, 73 percent of my survey participants included "everything is missions" in their top three choices. One in five respondents said that an all-inclusive attitude toward missions is "almost universal," and an additional two-thirds said it is "quite common." Forty-three percent feel it "very much" impacts believers' engagement with missions, and another third said it has "somewhat" of an impact. Overall, this perception tied with the idea that "missions is important but not primary" for the highest prevalence score and was rated second for impact on the North American church.

I also observed a difference between the groups of respondents. Missions agency staff and board members scored the perception that "everything we do is missions" significantly higher on impact than church members or leaders. Missionaries who have been on the field for fewer than six years also gave it higher impact scores than missionaries who have served longer. This suggests it may be a growing trend that stands out more to missionaries who raised support more recently. Overall, every survey group identified an all-inclusive view of missions as both common and concerning.

> **"The new missions pastor of a longtime supporting church introduced the theme, 'We're all missionaries and we're all in this together!' Within eighteen months they could no longer support their missions budget and had to cut most of their commitments."**
>
> ~ MISSIONARY ~

WHY THE EFFORT TO REDEFINE MISSIONS?

The push to broaden the meaning of missions to include any form of gospel-motivated good work is generally well intended. We want to reinforce the reality that everything we say, do, and think should glorify God. As Paul instructed us, "Whatever you do, whether in word or deed, do it all in the name of the Lord Jesus, giving thanks to God the Father through him" (Col. 3:17). In our desire to dignify everyday activities, we leverage the "spiritual prestige" of missions. Another reason for broadening the scope of missions is to motivate each other to share the gospel at every opportunity. There are aspects of the missionary task that all of us can do in just about any setting. We can build relationships with nonbelievers, share our faith, mentor and disciple those who respond, and welcome them into a church family. We might intend to benefit both local and foreign ministry efforts by equating these opportunities and responsibilities with missions.

> "I think there are dangers on both sides here. If missions is everything then the distinctions of missionary endeavors can be lost. If missions isn't integrated into the ministry philosophy of the church then we will be missing the mark as well."
>
> ~ CHURCH LEADER ~

A third motivation may be that we want everyone to have a sense of ownership and excitement for the Great Commission task. The long-term, faraway, cross-cultural part of the Great Commission should still feel relatable to the whole body of Christ. We don't want believers to feel detached from our missions efforts, so we emphasize everyone's important role. After a while, "everyone has an important role to play" can morph into "everyone is a missionary" and then "everything we do is missions."

An inclusive approach to missions may prevent people's view of missions from becoming too narrow. After all, the remotest, hardest, scariest places in the world aren't the only ones that matter. More and more, there are members of unreached people groups in our own communities here in the West. Not long ago, I struck up a conversation with the young lady cutting my hair at a local shop. Her name was Galia, and to my surprise she was a Tatar from Kazan, Russia. The Tatars are Russia's largest unreached people group, numbering about six million. Meeting Galia in my own neighborhood reminded me what a privilege it is to live in this era of history. It has never been easier to meet and share the gospel with someone from an unreached people group. If it's true that everything we do can glorify God and virtually any Christian can interact with someone who is unreached, what distinguishes missions from every other type of God-glorifying ministry?

DISTINCTIONS AND GENERALITIES

I believe that ministry within our own cultural context can be valuable without being missions. Global blessing through the gospel of Christ is the overarching theme of the Bible and the primary task of the church, but cross-cultural pioneering work is not the *only* task of the church. After all, the Great Commission is not the only mandate in Scripture. Jesus also endorsed the Great Commandment to love God and one another. Cross-cultural outreach does not represent the entirety of how God is glorified. The preparation of the bride of Christ for her wedding day involves many activities. It's okay if not everything we do is missions. It's not okay to *not* do missions.

> "Those that are not engaged in missions to the unreached are probably not living like a missionary where they are, either, regardless of what they believe theologically about missions."
>
> ~ MISSIONARY~

Holding to a clear, specific definition of missions does not exclude people from engaging in the full picture of what God has in mind for them. Defining missions as sending out workers to advance the gospel and make disciples cross-culturally in places

> **"All good work done worshipfully brings glory to God and blessing to those around us, but not all good work brings salvific blessing as the nations believe."**
>
> ~ MISSIONARY ~

that have very little church presence still allows infinite scope for the involvement of the whole body of Christ and for great creativity and imagination in how we engage as individuals. Because the Great Commission task is so huge and complex, we can play very different roles. We have thousands of people groups to reach. The possibilities of how God might use us to do that are endless. One of those possibilities is that we might become missionaries ourselves, going to today's "Ninevehs" as modern Jonahs (hopefully a little more willingly). But there are many other ways to participate. The global task belongs to everyone.

The danger is that in our well-meaning efforts to include and motivate everyone to live for Christ, we can lose sight of the big-picture goal of global worship. God's purpose for His church is for us to glorify Him by becoming more Christlike while we make obedient disciples of every people group on earth. However broad the list of activities we include under the term *missions*, each one should connect back to this ultimate purpose. Otherwise, we may find ourselves running off in all directions, metaphorically relying on carrots and ignoring our radar.

GENERICIZING MISSIONS

Evangelism is sharing the gospel with the people around us. Discipleship is bringing new believers to maturity. Missions is the intentional process of crossing cultural, linguistic, and (often) geographic barriers to carry out these activities. I believe that our

God is worthy to be worshiped in every one of the languages He has designed and by the redeemed of every ethnic group He has created. The church is responsible to pursue that mission with passion, prayer, perseverance, and faith.

The problem with redefining missions more broadly is that it dilutes our focus on an important dimension of what Christ has commanded us to do. We can only talk about concepts that we have vocabulary for. The language of the jungle tribe I grew up in, Sawi, has fewer than three thousand root words. For comparison, the average adult knows fifteen to twenty thousand root words in their first language.[3] Sawi people have lots of words relating to sago harvesting and to lighting and maintaining fires because those activities were historically so important to their survival. They have few (if any) words related to geopolitics, aerodynamics, real estate, or money management, much less quantum theory. In Sawi, any amount above three is simply "many." In centuries past, they didn't need to count to "seventy-six" or describe the rotational velocity of a planet. Every people group speaks with specificity about the topics that are important to them, but only generally about other subjects.

> "This is one of those areas where something good (witnessing, serving others, etc.) gets in the way of truly following the full heart of the Great Commission."
>
> ~ MISSIONARY ~

If missions is important to us, we need appropriate vocabulary to talk about it. God's purpose for His church is not just to redeem a lot of people, but to redeem people who represent, in a way that the apostle John could recognize from a distance, every single ethnolinguistic group on earth (Rev. 7:9). Jesus gave us the specific task of discipling the world, not just general instructions to be good people. Any task is easier to accomplish if we know what we are trying to do and have words to describe it.

As a global church, we won't disciple all the nations if we are content to only serve our neighbors. According to one recent estimate, more than 80 percent of the unbelievers alive today do not personally know a follower of Christ.[4] Our current communities make up only a portion of the world that we are meant to influence. That means hundreds of millions of people still have almost no access to the gospel in a language and cultural framework that they understand. This is the "hard work" before the harvest that Jesus spoke of when He challenged the thinking of His disciples after revealing Himself to the Samaritan woman at the well (John 4:38). Many people still live where there are no churches and speak languages into which no Scripture has ever been translated. We won't reach those peoples through organic growth. Without a strategic focus on world missions, we can go on making more disciples, but it's unlikely they will be from every language, tribe, and tongue.

> "If our definition is so broad that baking cookies for kids in the neighborhood is considered missions, then engaging in cross-cultural missions will naturally be diminished."
>
> ~CHURCH LEADER~

VOCABULARY MATTERS

In 1907, the American Thermos Bottle Company launched a marketing campaign to popularize its vacuum-insulated bottles. They succeeded so spectacularly that "thermos" became a household word. The problem was, by the early 1920s, competitors were using the term "thermos" to describe *their* vacuum-insulated bottles as well. And so began the battle for the trademark, which included multiple lawsuits, changing the name of the business to the American Thermos *Products* Company, and launching Thermos-branded tents and stoves in an effort to prove that "thermos" was not a generic word for vacuum bottles.[5] But it was too late. In 1963 a court deemed that the term "had entered the public domain beyond recall."[6]

> "If everyone is a missionary where they are, then no one needs to go anywhere. Everyone would just 'bloom where they are planted' while half the world remains a spiritual desert."
>
> ~ MISSIONARY ~

Thermos is not the only corporate brand to fall victim to its own success. "Escalator," "laundromat," and "zipper" all used to be trademarks.[7] Believe it or not, a company called Sealed Air Corporation still holds the rights to "Bubble Wrap," Wham-O Inc. owns "Hula Hoop," and Sony is hanging on to "Memory Stick."[8] Velcro went as far as producing a music video urging us to refer to generic versions of their product as "hook and loop,"[9] but I doubt that's going to catch on.

A Pioneers board member once cautioned me, "I don't think you are going to be able to take back the word *missions*." Even if he's right, which he may be, we still need to speak with clarity about the theological and cross-cultural dimensions of our calling. That means using appropriate terminology to avoid confusion. We make these kinds of adjustments all the time in other settings.

Missions jargon is often misinterpreted in countries and cultures outside the West. Descriptive expressions like "emissary" and "gospel ambassador" are helpful alternatives to "missionary" in some contexts. Whatever terminology we use, we need to beware of the current trend to broaden traditional missions vocabulary beyond recognition. When missions is everything and everyone is a missionary, we struggle to find words to identify the people who invest their lives in long-term efforts to cross linguistic and cultural boundaries in order to make disciples in people groups that do not yet have a gospel witness. The church needs such people, and we have to call them something. If we confuse or generalize our vocabulary, we forfeit our ability to speak with precision.

> "If missions is treated as just another program, then lay members will not view it as their prerogative to get involved unless they perceive a special call."
>
> ~CHURCH LEADER~

Defining missions specifically as cross-cultural disciplemaking among the unreached does not relegate other ministries to second-class status. Instead, it allows us to speak with clarity about our responsibility to take the gospel to every people group on earth. Reserving the term "missionary" for people with special training and experience in cross-cultural ministry does not make everyone else a second-class Christian. It does help us know who to send into ministry situations that require specialized skills.

The Great Commission is a difficult assignment that we don't have the authority to redefine. As Christopher Little puts it, "the personal aspirations of God's servants are not what determine the mission of the church, but rather the eternal needs of the lost."[10] Finishing the task of getting the gospel across cultural boundaries to the unreached peoples of the world requires that we marshal significant willpower and resources over a sustained period of time. By labeling every ministry as missions, we could inadvertently jeopardize our goal of reaching the vast diversity of people God intends to redeem.

DON'T OVERDO IT

In early 2021, a Belgian farmer moved a large rock out of the way of his tractor as he plowed his field. It turned out that the bothersome stone marked Belgium's border with France, established in 1820 after Napoleon's defeat at Waterloo. The farmer inadvertently moved the border line by about two meters, making Belgium a little bigger and France a little smaller. The French, unsurprisingly, were not particularly pleased.[11] This is one example of how geopolitical borders sometimes have very little relevance to people's lives. To the farmer, it was simply an inconvenient rock.

While broadening our definition of missions can undermine our focus on our mandate, we can also make the opposite error and define missions too narrowly. Sometimes we equate missions with crossing geographical or national boundaries and think of a missionary exclusively as someone who lives overseas. While much cross-cultural ministry is also international, the ethnolinguistic emphasis of the Great Commission prevents us from defining missions in such strictly geopolitical terms. People groups are distinguished by language, culture, and heritage.

Defining missions based on people groups rather than geography means that not everyone who ministers in a foreign country is involved in missions, and some people serving in cross-cultural ministry in their own communities *are* doing missions. Some Christians move internationally to minister to people from their home culture living abroad. Others travel abroad to care for the needy with no meaningful gospel connection or church development impact. If such ministries do not contribute to cross-cultural discipleship or church multiplication, they may be laudable activities and part of the bigger kingdom picture, but they fall outside the biblical scope of missions. Conversely, many missionaries work in their home countries serving immigrant, refugee, and other unreached communities, crossing cultures without ever crossing a border. The point isn't where you live, it's whether your primary role is discipling one or more of the many unreached peoples God created for His glory.

THE BOTTOM LINE

On a technical level, when you delete a document on your computer, you aren't erasing the content itself. You're erasing the file name and the navigation markers that allow the computer to find that content. Eventually a particular file may be overwritten by other data, but in the meantime, it persists on your hard drive in nameless oblivion. Without a name and pathway to access the file, from the computer's perspective, it ceases to exist.[12] Let's not let global missions suffer the same fate. Few Christians, no matter how inclusive their definition of missions, would argue against evangelizing the world. No one sets out to delete cross-cultural missions from the agenda of the church. But if we generalize its name beyond recognition, we may effectively erase the concept. That would be a massive loss for both the unreached and the church.

Our global missions calling is a privilege, not a burden. As J. Campbell White wrote, "Nothing can wholly satisfy the life of Christ within his followers except the adoption of Christ's purpose toward the world He came to redeem. Fame, pleasure and riches are but husks and ashes in contrast with the boundless and abiding joy of working with God for the fulfillment of

His eternal plans."[13] The church is strongest and most beautiful when it is most focused on accomplishing the purpose for which it was commissioned. Jesus not only commanded the church to make disciples of the nations, but He also designed the church specifically for that task. God's people will never be fully satisfied unless we lift up our eyes to the harvest and then take our place alongside our brothers and sisters, laboring with joy on behalf of the not-yet-saved.

Defining missions according to the Great Commission mandate does not limit us to only one type of ministry or relegate other ministries to second class. Rather, it frees us to apply the full resources of the entire global church to the task that our Lord appointed for us. An undefined task is difficult to finish. If you feel like you are drifting in a fog of vagueness regarding your purpose as a Christian, don't be discouraged. Switch on your radar. Lift up your eyes to the harvest, survey the landscape, and ask your heavenly Father to show you how you can join Him in bringing blessing to the nations. He delights to give us glimpses of His redemptive power at work in the world and in us. If we understand our mission, then we can better align our priorities and activities with God's plan. Together, we can look forward to crossing the finish line and hearing our Lord Himself say, "Well done, good and faithful servants."

> "This perception reduces the role of the North American Christian to providing for their family, serving their local church, and being a witness within their local sphere. God has an additional, global layer of service and witness in mind for each member of His global family."
>
> ~ MISSIONARY ~

DISCUSSION QUESTIONS

1. How have you heard the words "missions" and "missionary" used? In what ways does changing the meaning of these terms reshape our understanding of the Great Commission task? Would you say they are being preserved, redefined, replaced, or broadened?

2. What alternative terms do you think might be suitable substitutes for "missions" and "missionary"?

3. Are you drawn toward a concept of missions that includes every type of work for the kingdom of God? If so, why?

4. Have you considered the importance of crossing cultural and linguistic boundaries as a part of the Great Commission? Have you ever felt drawn to do so yourself?

4

MISSIONS COMPETES AGAINST EVERYTHING ELSE

Regardless of the particular work God has for each of us to do, the one aim of us all in doing our particular job for the Lord must be the evangelization of the whole world.

— G. ALLEN FLEECE

> **Perception 4:** Pursuing missions comes at a cost to other important ministries. A global focus reduces our local impact.

If the overarching task of the church in this age is to worship and obey Christ by making disciples throughout the world, and if missions is defined as an intentional and sustained effort to cross cultural and linguistic barriers in pursuit of that goal, then how does missions relate in practical terms to other activities and expressions of ministry? Is cross-cultural missions the only ministry that matters? Should we prioritize it at the expense of other important things? Our time, money, and energy are all limited, both as individuals and as church congregations, and we often feel pulled in different directions. Nearby needs and opportunities abound, and they can seem more urgent and more solvable than faraway global problems.

We've noted that defining missions specifically as cross-cultural disciple-making does not have to devalue other roles and ministries. It can still feel, however, that missions competes against those other ministries for resources. We only have so many evenings a week to spend either praying for the unreached or mentoring at-risk youth. Should we give toward a Bible translation project or to our local crisis pregnancy center? With so many needs in our own communities, how do we balance competing priorities? We can't support every cause, so we look at our options, pray for wisdom, make our choices, and trust God to take care of the rest.

The cost of pursuing missions isn't just a matter of time and resources. Fundamentally, it is a matter of people. As Jesus noted, the laborers are few (Luke 10:2). It is one thing to advocate for hypothetical missionaries to reach the lost. It is much harder to drop your grandchildren off at an airport on their way to the other side of the world. Missionaries who go out to fulfill the "ends of the earth" dimension of the Great Commission are sorely missed by the families, friends, and churches they leave behind. Effective cross-cultural disciple-making requires godly, mature believers, and not many churches think they have a surplus of such people. So do we pursue missions at the expense of our local churches? Does God ask us to choose the unreached over our families? Are we to meet physical needs or preach truth?

THE BINARY TRAP

When we are under stress, we tend to think in binary categories. We can go or stay. Give or save. Focus local or go global. Simplifying the options can help us cope with a complex world, but it can also reflect what Stephen Covey calls a *scarcity mentality* and make us susceptible to extreme and unnecessary pendulum shifts.[1] As Robertson McQuilkin observed in relation to balancing scriptural truths, "It seems easier to go to a consistent extreme than to stay at the center of biblical tension."[2] Easier, but not better. In many areas of life, maturity means holding seemingly competing truths in appropriate tension.

> "Churches that prioritize local social justice and mercy ministries resent being looked down on for these priorities by more missions-minded churches."
>
> ~ MISSIONARY ~

We often think of ministry possibilities like a typical intersection. If one light is green, the other will be red. If we move forward with one option or prioritize one group of people, we must reject or press pause on the alternatives. We can't do everything, so we must choose between our needs and the needs of the unreached, between home culture ministry and international missions, between evangelism and meeting physical needs. But what if we adopt an *abundance mentality* instead of a scarcity mentality? What if an active global ministry culture actually enhances our local impact? Perhaps we can think of these decisions as less like a four-way intersection and more like a roundabout.

Americans typically don't like roundabouts, although they are actually one of our important contributions to the world of transportation. The first circular intersection designed for motorized vehicles was Columbus Circle in New York City, opened in 1905. Well-functioning roundabouts are demonstrably safer, cheaper, and more efficient than four-way intersections. They do not require electricity to operate, they need little upkeep, traffic never stops moving, and it is impossible to have a head-on or T-bone collision because cars move at an angle to one another.[3]

Despite all these advantages, roundabouts didn't catch on in America. Vehicles flew into intersections at dangerous speeds, weaved through traffic, and crashed into each other. In between accidents, roundabouts jammed up with cars until no one could move. By the 1950s, most Americans concluded that intersections should be binary. A lot of us still think that.[4]

If you are the rare American who likes roundabouts, you have the British to thank. In 1966, they figured out what was going wrong. According to the original design of traffic circles, entering cars had the right-of-way, so drivers charged in at high speed without paying attention to vehicles already circling. Once inside, they had to both watch for their exit and avoid incoming drivers. If traffic was heavy, the entire circle filled up with cars and came to a standstill. The British realized they needed to reverse the right-of-way, giving priority to the cars inside the intersection. Entering vehicles then had to pause and make sure there was space for them. Circulating drivers could focus on exiting safely rather than dodging incoming cars. Once the correct right-of-way was established, capacity went up by 10 percent and crashes went down by almost half. Americans still took a lot of convincing. We didn't build any more roundabouts until 1990.[5]

The story of the traffic circle is an example of coordination for the greater good of everyone. The drivers inside the circle aren't more important than those outside it, but there has to be a prioritized sequence in order for everyone to get where they're going. Everyone benefits, even though incoming cars may have to slow down momentarily to find a gap. The difference between an efficient driving experience and total gridlock is the application of appropriate right-of-way rules.

It's not a perfect metaphor, but we can apply some of the same principles to the tension between global missions and other ministry opportunities in our home culture context. The goal is for the whole system to work well and for everyone to benefit so that the overall objective is realized. Because the Great Commission includes, and even emphasizes, the discipleship of *all* peoples, the church must ensure that the cross-cultural dimension of ministry is honored. Perhaps, in one sense, we can picture it as giving the "right-of-way" to those with the least access to the gospel. It isn't that the unreached in faraway places are more important than our neighbors. It's that getting the gospel to them will require a lot more intentional effort from the church. Most of us don't need to dramatically rearrange our lives in order to share the gospel with our neighbors. But a significant number of us *will* have to rearrange our lives to communicate that message to the 3.5 billion people alive today who don't yet have access to Bibles, churches, or followers of Jesus. For most Christians, the global dimension is the easiest to neglect.

When it comes to ministry decisions, we need to resist simplistic, binary conclusions and focus on nurturing a healthy ecosystem so that we keep the big picture of the Great Commission in view and pursue it actively. If we embrace a biblical vision of reaching every people group, then we can bring other parts of our lives into alignment with that overarching purpose, including ministry to our families and our communities.

MISSIONS VS. MY NEEDS AND MY FAMILY

Many followers of Jesus, sadly, lack any sense of personal mission. We just live day by day, barreling full speed into roundabouts, surprised and annoyed when we find others in our way. It can feel like increased involvement in global missions would be a detriment to our personal and family well-being.

If you're like me, your natural tendency is to let your focus drift inward as life becomes more complicated. Under stress we lose our peripheral vision. If I'm not careful, the Christian life can begin to feel like it is about me, my sanctification, my prosperity, my safety, and my family's spiritual growth. Our personal and family needs are real and constantly changing. We need to attend to them. The challenge is, there is no clear line of demarcation between responsibly providing for ourselves and the people we love and getting caught up in the pursuit of bigger houses, nicer vacations, and greater financial security. None of those things is necessarily wrong, but they can pull our eyes down to focus on our own comfort and safety, causing us to lose sight of God's greater purposes for us and our families. The lure of materialism may be especially evident in Western culture, but I suspect it's true for people almost anywhere. As Christians, we all need to scrutinize our lifestyles with the Great Commission in mind.

Without doubt, our personal walk with God is a major arena of God-glorifying, transformational activity. Yet, personal sanctification and the discipleship of the unreached don't have to compete for our attention. The two are inseparable, although right-of-way matters. Abram was called out of his comfort zone into a journey of obedience. When he left Ur, he didn't even know his final destination (Heb. 11:8). He learned to live by faith as God gradually revealed His plan to bless the world through his descendants. The same will happen for us as we join God's global redemptive mission.

If you sincerely want to deepen your walk with God, the best place to do it is on a journey of obedience. We grow in our faith, confidence, and fruitfulness as we seek to understand the heart of God and join Him in His mission in the world. Opting for the perceived safety of the sidelines is not going to accelerate your spiritual growth. Pursuing your own sanctification without participating in the Great Commission is like waiting to practice the piano until you finish learning the song. It won't work. You learn as you practice.

And what about our families? At my daughter's graduation celebration at a Christian high school, one graduate after another announced their college and career plans to enthusiastic applause. As I recall, not a single student talked about gospel impact or ministry involvement. I am all for successful careers and well-paying jobs, but what about the kingdom dimension? Was it just assumed? I wonder how we are conveying an eternal value system to the next generation. What greater gift can we give the children we love than the assurance that their lives are part of a grand, God-glorifying mission to bless the peoples of the world? What more could we hope for than to see them devote their lives to Great Commission service in whatever ways God opens up for them?

Ask God to fashion you and your church into conduits of His blessing to the nations. In our increasingly self-absorbed and safety-conscious culture, missions engagement often feels either irrelevant or risky. And it is definitely risky, at least as the world sees things. The enemy does not want us to be active, en-gaged global Christians. He is trying to distract, discourage, and frighten us. Let's not fall for his tricks. We do not have to choose between taking care of ourselves and our families or helping to reach the world. Our personal needs and God's big-picture plan do not represent a binary choice. There is no better way to grow our faith and love our families than to participate together in the discipleship of the nations.

MISSIONS VS. THE LOCAL CHURCH

At the Christian college I attended many years ago, I sensed a simmering "holy war." On the one side were the students preparing for the pastorate, Bibles in hand, sporting a growing mastery of Greek, theology, and church polity. Arrayed against them were the aspiring missionaries, brandishing our linguistic, anthropological, and evangelistic credentials. Which side would win? We joked about it, but sometimes the tension felt real.

> "Increasingly, churches in the US seem to feel that it is almost poor stewardship to divert resources from needs in the local community to supporting Western missionaries."
>
> ~ MISSIONARY ~

It is possible to be a lifelong, contributing member of a church and engage in meaningful local ministry without ever giving much thought to Christ's command to make disciples of all nations. Most churches have bigger visions for local ministry than their staff, budget, and volunteers can carry out. It can be tempting to think we should tackle nearby needs first before taking on the rest of the world. A 2018 study found that less than half of churchgoing Christians in America were even familiar with the term "Great Commission."[6]

With a little creativity, we can rationalize our way out of a global perspective and back to binary thinking. For example, Jesus said that His disciples would be "witnesses in Jerusalem, and in all Judea and Samaria, and to the ends of the earth" (Acts 1:8). Christians sometimes interpret this as a sequential process: first reach your immediate circle of influence, then pursue ministries to your Judea and Samaria (nearby communities and cultures), and then, if you still have time and energy, go to the ends of the earth. Or, some people read it as a list of options. As long as I'm involved in "my Jerusalem," I don't need to be concerned about the rest of the world. Denny Spitters points out a flaw in this thinking: "Jesus was not telling His disciples to start at home and to move on when they got that done. The disciples were Galileans. Jerusalem was not their home; it was a strategic launch point to the nations."[7]

I think one reason God strategically positioned the disciples in Jerusalem was that He was about to flood the city with Jewish pilgrims from all across the Mediterranean region. Thousands of people were saved through the disciples' ministry at Pentecost and carried the gospel with them when they returned home. Do we evaluate our church activities according to how strategic they are for reaching the nations? When we envision new local ministries, do we consider how to maximize their worldwide impact?

One of the gifts that the church in the West can give to the global Christian community is our organized way of planning and executing projects, including our response to God's Great Commission call. In local churches, this has often taken the form of committees, budgets, events, and protocols. We have set up systems of sustained sending and disciplined giving that have greatly benefited the cause. One danger, however, may be our tendency to relegate global missions to "program" status. Over time we can compartmentalize the missions program and perceive it as belonging only to a certain group of activists. While programs and structures have their important place, we must keep explaining and emphasizing the big picture and keep lifting our eyes both to God's Word and to God's world. In our roundabout metaphor, it means establishing a right-of-way for ministry to the unreached by routinely asking, "How does this particular activity contribute to discipling *all* the nations?" A Great Commission mindset is far more than a program. It is a culture, a worldview, that energizes and aligns all that we do.

If we lift our eyes to the worldwide task that Jesus gave us, every area of our lives will become more vibrant, not less so. As God's church, we can give the less fortunate of our communities more than just resources and time. We also have a God-given vision and sense of purpose that the world around us desperately needs. As we mentor at-risk youth, serve the homeless, and support single mothers in our communities, we can disciple those who believe and encourage them to impact the world for Christ. We can design our children's programs to disciple our kids in such a way that they think about the whole world and perhaps are even inspired to pursue ministry among the unreached. We can love our church members and our communities best by pointing them to the pursuit of God's worldwide glory.

In my own life, I have found that my commitment to impacting the world for Christ makes me a better husband, father, friend, boss, employee, and neighbor. The more I commit to knowing God and participating in His plan to bless the nations, the more I reflect His Son to people around me, perhaps without even realizing it. But if I focus only on the immediate needs and opportunities of the day, I'm unlikely to become a blessing to the nations by accident. Reaching the world takes intentionality.

My observation is that the same could be said about churches. Churches that have a missions focus are centrifuges for the gospel. They send people out and keep growing, changing the world near and far for the glory of God. Churches that have a vision beyond their immediate surroundings tend to also have vibrant local ministries. But not all churches that focus on their own communities also have a global vision.

If it sometimes feels as if God is asking us to sacrifice the health and local impact of our churches for the sake of people we've never met whose names we can't pronounce, we can take comfort from the example of the church at Antioch. In the middle of a fruitful season of local ministry, the Holy Spirit instructed them to release two of their best leaders, Barnabas and Paul, into ministry in far-off lands (Acts 13). I doubt the Antioch church had finished evangelizing and transforming their city. There was still much to be done. However, God had a bigger plan for them than just reaching their own community. By giving up two of their most experienced leaders, the Antioch church stepped onto the global stage and changed the course of history. Through their sacrifice, Antioch church members played a vital role in reaching the Mediterranean world with the gospel. What a spectacular privilege! Most Christians alive today probably owe our spiritual heritage in some degree to that act of obedience. As Barnabas and Paul sailed away, other leaders emerged and the church continued to grow. Responding to God's call is always in our best interest, even if it doesn't immediately feel that way.

One of the most common scriptural metaphors for the church is the human body. Every part plays a unique and important role.

When one member suffers or is absent, it affects the whole. Imbalanced churches that have little concern for the deeper Christian life or for reaching their neighbors will help no one. On the other hand, a strong ministry at home, both within the congregation and in the surrounding community, can be vulnerable if it is not connected to long-term global impact. There is danger in not having a robust and complementary vision for both healthy local bodies and strategic outreach to the nations. The two are meant to thrive together.

Missions and other aspects of church life don't have to be in conflict. No doubt many good things competed for Paul's attention as he planted a ring of churches around the eastern Mediterranean. He wrote more than a dozen books of the New Testament, all of them addressed to believers. He had a huge role in laying the theological foundations of the early church. He discipled younger men like Timothy and Titus, sending them to strengthen the churches he planted. In Galatians he describes his eagerness to "remember the poor" (Gal. 2:10). He organized a major financial gift from the Gentiles of Macedonia and Achaia to the believers in Jerusalem (Rom. 15:25). Paul healed the sick, encouraged the weak, and pastored the pastors of the early church.

Yet, amid all this intense ministry to believers, he never lost his big-picture drive to keep breaking new ground in the unreached world. He wrote to the church in Rome, "It has always been my ambition to preach the gospel where Christ was not known, so that I would not be building on someone else's foundation" (Rom. 15:20). He even says, "there is no more place for me to work in these regions" (Rom. 15:23). That's an astonishing claim that reflects the heart of a pioneer. Expanding the perimeter of gospel influence was Paul's overarching priority, and he diligently served the church with that goal in mind. Paul's focus on the proclamation of the gospel did not prevent him from caring for the needs of the believers in his homeland. He did not choose missions over the church. Instead, he lived and breathed missions into the church. And while Paul may have had a unique apostolic calling, there is much we can learn from his integrated approach to ministry.

The church is custom designed for both local and global impact. The clearer our view of the big picture (which includes a right-of-way for those currently without access to the gospel), the more the body of Christ will benefit at home, abroad, and everywhere in between. If we only focus on ourselves or our neighbors, everything begins to jam up and our ministries may eventually stall out. We may think we are protecting ourselves by focusing only on our local communities, but we are actually endangering our churches by depriving them of meaningful engagement in God's global redemption plan. God doesn't intend for world missions to compete against other initiatives in the church. He intends for missions to help inspire and motivate all the other dimensions of church life, infusing them with a global perspective. If your church seems to be jammed up with little enthusiasm and little growth, consider whether you have the right-of-way the wrong way round. Maybe there's an opportunity to lift your eyes a little higher.

MISSIONS VS. SOCIAL JUSTICE AND DEVELOPMENT

What about the tension between meeting the physical needs of the lost and evangelizing them? Between pursuing justice and preaching the gospel? Should we focus primarily on physical needs, or spiritual ones? It's a question not only for international missions, but for the church wherever we happen to be. It relates to questions of genuine compassion, but also to sociopolitical dynamics and theological perspectives. Is hell real? Do people really need to be "saved"? What does it mean to "preach" and to "make disciples"? I often hear a statement attributed to St. Francis of Assisi, "Preach the gospel at all times. When necessary, use words."[8] For me, using words is the hardest part, so this counsel sounds like a welcome relief! But does it reflect God's priorities and His instructions to the church?

> "American culture has shamed the church into doing local social work instead of 'proselytizing,' which now has a very negative connotation."
>
> ~ MISSIONARY ~

Jesus endorsed not just the Great Commission, but also the Great Commandment—"Love the Lord your God" and "Love your neighbor as yourself" (Mark 12:30–31). He didn't pit them against each other, and neither should we. Our responsibility is to both demonstrate and communicate love, and love demands that we evangelize the world. God's perspective and the priority of the gospel are beautifully described by Robertson McQuilkin:

> If all people on earth could prosper and be given a college education, full employment prevailed, all injustice and warfare ceased, and perfect health prevailed, but people remained alienated from God, his father-heart would still be broken. His *first* priority for alienated beings is reconciliation to himself. . . . If utopia could be created for time but human beings were lost for eternity, the Father's heart could never be satisfied.[9]

Articulating the gospel is not the only way we can show love, but it's an absolutely crucial way.

Aligning ourselves with God's priorities allows us to accomplish the more tangible help that we long to bring to a hurting world. Society changes when hearts change. Jesus had no problem preaching the good news of the kingdom while ministering to people's physical needs. He asked, "What good will it be for someone to gain the whole world, yet forfeit their soul?" (Matt. 16:26). Jesus ministered to the whole person without neglecting their greatest need of all. Emphasizing the gospel message doesn't mean that we don't care about human suffering. John Piper stated it eloquently at the Lausanne Conference in 2010: "We Christians care about all suffering, especially eternal suffering."[10] We preach the gospel because we care too much to let people live and die without eternal hope. If you really believe in social transformation, you should be fully committed to global missions.

The gospel has always advanced in lockstep with concrete demonstrations of the love of God. A vast number of hospitals, educational institutions, and social breakthroughs worldwide can be traced to the work of missionaries. In a tribal context, my missionary parents developed an alphabet, taught people to read, and secured peace between warring villages. The tribes in that area tended to be small because so many people died of disease and warfare. A man in his forties was considered old. My mother probably saved a life a week, on average, through her medical ministry. My own ministry years later on a team in an urban Muslim context involved numerous development and compassion ministries.

As we go to the world, God uses us to liberate, educate, heal, and enrich many, but our most revolutionary offering is the gospel. Jesus died on the cross to pay the penalty for the sins of the world. If that message isn't articulated clearly, it will quickly be lost. McQuilkin summarizes well: "Although there are many ways to express the Great Commandment, its purest manifestation comes when God's people persuade others to love God. . . . Indeed, when it comes to the lost, the best way to obey the Great Commandment is to live by the Great Commission."[11]

The Great Commission represents the culmination of all that Jesus did and taught, not an afterthought. The world needs to know that Christ has reconciled us to our Creator through His death and resurrection (Col. 1:21–23). This reality leads logically and directly to worldwide evangelism. We want all people, everywhere, to have an opportunity to hear, believe, and live according to that truth.

THE BOTTOM LINE

Rather than being one good thing we do at the expense of everything else, glorifying God by being His witnesses to the world should be our overall, unifying theme. We won't all be missionaries, but we can all live with a missions mindset. There is a healthy and necessary tension between the local and global dimensions of our calling as God's people. If you're feeling that tension, you're probably in a good place. If you don't feel the tension, consider whether you've lost a vision for either your community or for the nations.

We don't have to live with a scarcity mentality, confined to binary options. God will provide the resources for the work He calls us to do. We can pursue synergy between ministry strategies rather than viewing them as competing priorities. Ministry to our neighbors and ministry to the unreached are both part of God's plan. The Great Commission implies a right-of-way for the unreached that simultaneously facilitates spiritual blessing for believers, our families, and our churches.

> "There appears to be a strong swing toward 'What can I do to help practically?' rather than 'This is the gospel. Repent and believe.'"
>
> ~ MISSIONARY ~

We pursue the Great Commission task because Jesus commanded it and because He is worthy of the worship of all peoples and cultures. That means that our efforts must extend to the unreached, the people with the least access to churches, believers, and the gospel. Our best opportunity for personal growth and true adventure is to engage in that global effort with a long-term big-picture mindset, no matter how it may play out practically in our individual circumstances. While it can feel risky or inconvenient, it will make our families and local churches healthier, transforming us into freshwater rivers rather than stagnant ponds. When we reach out to our neighbors and disciple them, they can then join us in reaching out to yet others, expanding our ability to impact the rest of the world.

The way to resolve the conflicts we feel between ministry options is to align our values with God's. Prioritizing will always be a challenge, but the Holy Spirit gives wisdom as we seek God's will through His Word and prayer. A coherent and integrated view of the church's responsibilities is good for everyone involved—individual Christians, local churches, the global church, and the unreached.

To grow in our spiritual maturity, we need to pursue the global task God has given us. To strengthen our churches, we must see them as a conduit of blessing to the nations. If we really love people and seek justice, we will be passionate about sharing the gospel. A competitive or dismissive spirit is counterproductive. It's like believing that carrots will allow you to see in the dark. Don't fall for the ruse. Turn on your radar, open the Scriptures, and fly with confidence, both locally and beyond. When the Lord returns or calls us home, may He find us enthusiastically going about our Father's business.

DISCUSSION QUESTIONS

1. What tensions do you personally feel as it relates to global missions?

2. How might a global mindset benefit your family, local ministry, and congregation?

3. How could an abundance mentality change the way you and your church make ministry decisions?

5

MISSIONS IS NOW SHORT TERM

Short term missions requires long term commitment.

— DAVID JOANNES

Perception 5: Churches don't need to send career missionaries anymore. They can send their members short term instead and still make a big impact.

In the late 1980s, I escaped the crowded Indonesian city where I lived to hike up a volcano on a small island and be refreshed by the quiet of rural life. I saw almost no one until I came upon a local Baskhara man plowing a rice paddy near the trail with a water buffalo. We struck up a conversation and soon he began to tell me stories about the more than forty countries he had visited. That's right, this rural farmer had seen far more of the world than I had at that point in my life. It turns out that young Baskhara men traditionally spend time traveling the world before they settle down at home to farm. This man had traded rice paddies and water buffalo for a job on a freighter and had visited Russia, Bulgaria, Turkey, and dozens of other places that I could only dream about.

That was more than thirty years ago, and the world has only grown more interconnected. We can now travel between almost any two airports on the planet in less than forty-eight hours. While transportation can still be challenging today, almost any journey looks less arduous when compared to the corresponding land or sea route that travelers faced a century ago. In 1910, for example, a second-class steamship fare between New York and England cost about fifty dollars,[1] which equates to roughly $1,500 in today's economy.[2] The speed record for crossing the Atlantic was 4.5 days.[3] Today I could fly to London after work on a Friday, take in the sights, hop over to Paris for a day, catch a red-eye home, and be back in the office Monday morning, all in less time and for less money than it would take the 1910 steamship to reach the docks at Liverpool.

What does our newfound mobility mean for missions? Physically going to the places where unreached people groups live no longer automatically requires a long-term commitment. In many cases, travel isn't even necessary. Increasingly, we can attend meetings, develop relationships, and contribute to projects virtually rather than in person. As technology develops, opportunities for Christians to be intensively involved in missions for a short period of time are multiplying.

When asked about the perception that short-term missions can replace long-term missions, almost half of our survey respondents answered that it is "quite common" or "almost universal." More than half said that the idea has "somewhat" or "very much" of an impact on the North American church. A third of church leaders and almost half of all field workers listed "missions is now short term" in their top three perceptions that hinder believers' engagement in missions. So how do short-term trips and virtual assignments fit into the Great Commission? Is it still strategic to send a few cross-cultural workers for long-term ministry when we can now send many more for shorter stints?

Short-term missions has definitely been on the rise over the last few decades. A 2012 Barna study found that 23 percent of evangelical Christians had participated in a short-term mission trip.[4] According to Dr. Robert Wuthnow, a researcher at Princeton University, US churches spend almost a third of their missions budget on short-term trips.[5] Some estimate that North American churches spend about four billion dollars on short-term trips every year.[6] And short-term missions is not just for teens. According to one study, in 2014 more than half of international volunteers for any cause were married adults, more than half had college degrees, and more than a third lived in households with annual incomes above $100,000.[7]

> "I get asked every year to host a short-term high school team, even the year when missionaries in our country were being targeted by ISIS terrorists. The places that host short-term teams suck the majority of the mission focus and funds away from harder, more unreached places."
>
> ~ MISSIONARY ~

Not every short-term experience is created equal. The rapid growth of both short-term missions and social media has triggered some backlash against "voluntourism," where young people go on trips mainly to have fun and be seen doing good, rather than out of a genuine desire to serve or to learn. Hopefully all thoughtful Christians can agree that such trips are generally unhelpful to global missions. Our main concern in this chapter is not whether short-term missions is good or bad, because it can be either. Our question here is whether, at their best, short-term

> "One church told me that they are all about local outreach and do short-term missions as a way of training people to do outreach back home."
>
> ~ MISSIONARY ~

trips or virtual experiences can replace long-term missionary work. Can a Western church have the same or greater impact on the unreached by investing in short-term missions as they can by supporting long-term missionaries? Is there still a need for missionaries to spend years living among the unreached, or is it now possible to accomplish the same thing by sending teams for a few weeks at a time?

THE CASE FOR LONG-TERM MISSIONS

An article from Desiring God makes a provocative assertion about short-term ministry: "Missions is the process of reaching unreached peoples with the Gospel, which requires intense language-learning, cultural study, and relationship-building. Short-term missions, therefore, does not exist."[8] In other words, the phrase "short-term missions" is an oxymoron. I am a big advocate for short-term missions, but I agree that the core of the Great Commission is discipleship, and discipleship is a long process. We can help someone begin or advance in their walk with the Lord in a short time frame, but we can't teach people all that Jesus commanded us in a few weeks or even months, especially through a translator, no matter how gifted or skillful we are. That means we must connect short-term missions (and all other ministry strategies) to the long-term big picture of God's global redemption plan.

A core tenet of the New Testament ministry model is life-on-life discipleship. Jesus lived with His disciples for three years, teaching them by word and example as they traveled, rested, ate, and argued. And this was after He had already spent thirty years learning the local language and culture! After Jesus' ascension, the apostles eventually spread out to other places, most of them dying violent deaths far from home as they sought to obey the Great Commission. There is no more profound communication of God's love than incarnational ministry alongside people who need the Lord. In most cultures—maybe all cultures—we pick up a lot more in terms of life change and behavior from what people model than from what they say.

Some aspects of love and learning can only be communicated by example over time. Similarly, cultures within the body of Christ can best learn from each other through sustained contact.

What about the apostle Paul? After he was sent out from the church at Antioch, the longest we have record of him staying in one place, other than prison, is his two years in Ephesus. Paul was constantly on the move. Was he a serial short-termer? We must keep in mind that Paul was a Roman citizen and fluent in the languages of most of the people he ministered to. He had the benefit of a deep awareness of the gospel recipients' context that modern short-termers usually lack. Some aspects of Paul's travels were undoubtedly cross-cultural (in Lystra and Derbe, for example), but it was all within a broad Roman context and Greek language. He wasn't ministering to

> **"It is difficult to correctly identify needs and develop appropriate actions without the long-term relationships associated with career missions. Short-term missions is often about being seen to do something and focuses on the one going, not the ones being served."**
>
> ~ MISSIONARY ~

the Aztec or the Zulu. This allowed him to have a major impact in a short period of time.

Despite Paul's often tight ministry time frames, we see evidence of his long-term mindset in the intensity with which he taught and trained. His approach to missions was wholehearted and lifelong. Even Paul's shorter stays were marked by the incarnational nature of his ministry. In Thessalonica, Paul and his coworkers "worked night and day in order not to be a burden to anyone" (1 Thess. 2:9). Believers had opportunity to closely observe Paul's "holy, righteous and blameless" lifestyle, and it strengthened them to withstand persecution (1 Thess. 2:10, 14–15).

Another expression of Paul's long-term mindset is the deep relationships he built. He developed pastoral relationships that left him heartbroken when he was separated from the churches or when they went astray (Acts 20:17, 36–38; 21:12–13; Gal. 4:19–20). He returned to strengthen the fragile churches he left behind and between visits he wrote letters and sent representatives. Because Paul always functioned within a team, his coworkers were able to do a lot of the long-term discipling (Apollos, Priscilla and Aquilla, Timothy, Titus, etc.). Paul modeled long-term ministry in a vast area of influence, not a pattern of disconnected short-term trips. In a sense he combined the best of both worlds, including both short-term and long-term dynamics.

Today, in places where the church has already taken root but is not yet strong enough to saturate a people group with the gospel, local believers are still asking for long-term missionaries to provide support, encouragement, and teaching. Long-term missionaries are also a blessing to their sending churches. They are a conduit for a local body to participate in the great work of God around the world. There is still much pioneering missions work to be done, and it will require sustained investment from the global body of Christ to see the remaining unreached peoples gather to worship our Lord. Discipleship is a process, not an event.

THE CASE FOR SYNERGY

If the core of missions is the discipling of the nations and discipleship is a long-term process, then missions must always be informed by a long-term mindset. That doesn't mean, however, that short-term ministry is without value. The two approaches do not have to compete. We can fund summer trips for college students *and* financially support career cross-cultural missionaries. Better yet, we can send those college students to encourage and learn from the missionaries we admire and support and from their partners. Short-term experiences (whether in person or virtual) are not a substitute for long-term disciple-making, but they can be a valuable part of a long-term missions strategy.

> "In the past, our church sent 1,800–2,000 people on 70–80 trips per year. We have not sent a commensurate number of long-term workers. Massive short-term success may hinder long-term engagement."
>
> ~ CHURCH LEADER ~

At Pioneers, we keep our focus on long-term, cross-cultural disciple-making ministry. As part of that overarching goal, we facilitate short-term trips for many students and young adults. We also have pathways designed for adult professionals who want to use their skills and expertise to contribute to global missions in a short-term time frame, either in person or virtually. These programs work together in support of our Great Commission efforts. They don't compete for resources and attention.

As we consider how and why to incorporate short-term ministry in our personal lives and our churches, we need to give each its proper priority. Some churches have made short-term missions their core strategy, with long-term missionaries sent out only when absolutely necessary. I propose that our core strategy should be long-term incarnational ministry, strengthened and bolstered by an array of complementary approaches such as short-term trips, strategic funding of partners, and virtual participation. We need diversity in our strategies to reach our one, universal goal: making obedient disciples of every people group on earth for the glory of God. Let's look at some of the ways that short-term missions can inspire and support long-term cross-cultural discipleship, and how the two approaches can work in synergy rather than competition.

Field Impact. Early on in our time on the field, my wife started a quilting business to help impoverished people in our urban community. As more and more people asked for employment, Arlene realized she was out of her depth. She had never actually made a quilt herself! We put out the word, and before long an award-winning quilter from Colorado volunteered to help. Linda traveled to Indonesia at her own expense to train a core group of quilters for two weeks. After Linda returned home, these expert quilters went on to train many more. The project eventually employed four hundred people, providing them with a marketable skill and a steady income while paving the way for the spread of the gospel. Because of her expertise and servant attitude, Linda's short-term investment in the ministry continued to bear spiritual fruit for decades. At the same time, Arlene was still there on-site helping to ensure that Linda's investment of time and expertise would withstand the test of time in the challenging local environment. This exciting story is recounted in more detail in Arlene's book, *Threads.*[9]

Visits from supporters and prayer partners can also be a real encouragement to weary missionaries. Paul experienced this benefit when the Philippian church sent Epaphroditus to care for his needs while he was imprisoned in Rome. Short-term missions was no exotic vacation for Epaphroditus. Paul says that he risked his life to support Paul's ministry (Phil. 2:25–30). Paul also sent many of his teammates on short visits to new or struggling churches. Tychicus, for example, carried Paul's letters of exhortation to the churches at Ephesus and Colossae (Eph. 6:21–22; Col. 4:7–8). These are great examples of synergy between a career missionary and missions-minded believers carrying out specific, short-term ministry tasks.

Participant Impact. Another way that short-term trips contribute to global missions is by their impact on the travelers. According to Barna, "three-quarters of trip-goers report that the experience changed their life in some way."[10] Barna's survey respondents credited the trips with increasing their awareness of others' struggles, poverty, and injustice, and helping them to grow in compassion, faith, spiritual understanding, and financial generosity.

A well-designed firsthand experience can be one of the best ways to feel connected with what God is doing among the unreached. It is hard to care about and pray for people whose lives we can't imagine and whose homes we can't find on a map. Reading statistics about the unreached is not the same as driving past village after village after village that has no church, no believers, and no access to the gospel. Church leaders, church members, and even teenagers can see, touch, feel, and breathe in God's passion for the unreached and carry a renewed vision for global ministry home with them.

One short-termer had been praying for an unreached people group for more than five years before visiting missionaries that her church supported. "I was excited to meet the people who I had been praying for this whole time," she explained. "You see pictures and you hear stories, but it's a different matter when you actually get to go." She woke up to the call to prayer, rode around the city on the back of a motorcycle, shopped in an open market, and visited a local family in their home. "I used all my five senses to be in that experience," she notes. "Riding on the motorcycle, I held out my hands over the ground and prayed for the city, and I felt like my prayers were part of the foundation of the church in that place." After returning home she found that her prayer life deepened and her giving felt more meaningful.

Church Impact. Seeing how people live and work and worship in other parts of the world gives us a broader perspective on both the vastness of the Great Commission task and the beautiful diversity of the global church. God changes people through short-term missions, and He changes churches through His people. Because believers who take short-term mission trips usually come home brimming with enthusiasm and stories, whole congregations can become more excited and informed about missions work they support. Churches can be inspired to pray more passionately, give more generously, and send out their own members as missionaries. It

> "It always helps to have local ambassadors for the global body."
>
> ~ MISSIONARY ~

is easier to engage in missions efforts from afar when you have walked through the harvest fields, not just heard about them.

Long-Term Mobilization Impact. Short-term trips can be a powerful catalyst for lifelong missions involvement, releasing more resources in the body of Christ for the discipleship of the nations. An effective trip highlights the need for cross-cultural discipleship and church planting ministry and challenges short-termers to consider their long term impact. Visitors to the field may see needs and opportunities that they never knew existed. Many missionaries point to short-term experiences as an influential factor in their decision to serve long term. At Pioneers, around 20 percent of participants in our short-term Edge program come back to join us as long-term workers. That doesn't include those who go on to join other organizations. Sixty-four percent of people who initially apply for mid-term trips (three months to one year) go on to serve with us long term. Almost everyone who applies for long-term service with Pioneers has been on a number of short-term trips as part of their journey of preparation. God obviously uses short-term missions.

> "I am grateful for short-term missions, as it can fuel a heart for long-term missions."
> ~ CHURCH LEADER ~

A short-term trip can also help to set realistic expectations of what field life is like, at least in a particular location. One cross-cultural worker described how a two-month exposure trip helped to shape his understanding of long-term ministry: "I realized that physical discomfort isn't a glorious sacrifice, that personal sin doesn't suddenly dissipate when it sees you've gone onto the mission field, and that many days are lonely or mundane. God was preparing me for reality!"

Leadership Impact. Pastors and elders have a huge influence over the agenda and culture of the churches they shepherd. Unfortunately, in some churches, individual members champion missions involvement with little support from their leadership. A short-term trip can help lift the eyes of pastors and elders from the busyness and challenges of local ministry to take in God's global harvest field. Almost all missions-minded churches are blessed with senior leadership who not only believe in the vision, but articulate it regularly from the pulpit and work actively to integrate a Great Commission mindset into the life and teaching of the congregation.

> "Many churches focus on short-term sending with little formal effort directed at sending long-term workers. I think it is often due to a lack of missions culture among church leaders. Perhaps this can be addressed by having more church leaders visit the mission field."
>
> ~ MISSIONARY ~

When church leaders make trips to the field and are exposed to the needs and examples of the indigenous church, they often become much more engaged. This is especially true when they participate in well-chosen and thoughtful trips to the field on a regular basis, rather than a single eye-opening experience. I suggest that every elder board include in their senior pastor's job description that they will take an international trip at least every two years. It will stimulate their missions passion and vision and remind them of an old truth: "Remember that your parish . . . is not your field. The field is the world. Your parish contains a force committed to you by God to train for him that he may reach the field which is the world."[11]

* * *

There are many ways in which a committed Christian, qualified for a particular task, can make a significant contribution to world missions in a limited amount of time. It's even possible to contribute to the Great Commission by vacationing in an exotic location. You can share your faith as you go, and workers in some countries run tourism businesses and can benefit when like-minded believers book vacations that help provide access to

> "A trip can whet one's appetite for what could be done and can give an appreciation for what all is involved in cross-cultural work."
>
> ~ MISSIONARY~

unreached communities. I would go so far as to say that some believers can make more of an impact for the gospel through strategic short-term missions than if they went long term themselves. The key word is *strategic*.

Arlene and I hosted a team of nine college students within our first few weeks in Indonesia. The visiting young people were transformed by the experience. They lived with local families and bonded so closely in a short time that more than seventy people came to the train station to say goodbye to them at the end of the summer.

Arlene and I benefited from the encouragement of English-speaking reinforcements and from the many relationships we were able to continue with local families after the students left. The Indonesian church was blessed because some of the students and their sending churches became long-term ministry partners. The sending churches were bolstered by the enthusiasm for the gospel and passion for the unreached that their young people brought home with them. One of the short-termers asked if she could stay on for an extra nine months. We agreed on the condition that her home church give their blessing. When she explained the situation and ministry opportunities to her missions pastor, he agreed that she should stay through the school year and the church would continue supporting her. At the end of the year she went home to reassess, earned a master's degree in Bible, and returned to Indonesia. She's still there, thirty-five years later, married to a local man and thriving in family and ministry. Two other members of that first team also returned to Indonesia for many years of fruitful ministry. I know from personal experience that short-term missions can contribute tremendously to the Great Commission. Those benefits do not, however, make it a substitute for the difficult long-term work that also needs to be done.

WHAT TO WATCH OUT FOR

For all their synergistic potential, there are ways short-term trips can go wrong, even if we mean well. Many missionaries have learned to be cautious from bad experiences. They envision teenagers bumbling through construction projects instead of employing local workers who need jobs and actually know how to build things. They cringe at the thought of culturally insensitive presentations of the gospel through translators and youth group trips that divert resources and personnel from long-term ministry. Mismanaged short-term

> "We were the only overseas missionaries at a missions weekend at a supporting church. We were not given any presentation time. We sat in the audience and listened to the church young people talk about their one-week experience in the country where we lived and worked."
>
> ~ MISSIONARY~

trips can also reinforce unhelpful stereotypes in the minds of both the receiving people and the short-termers. An Indonesian church leader once observed a group of young American short-termers and asked me how much the church had spent to send them. He wondered aloud how many local workers could have been helped or hired if they had simply sent the money instead.

Bad experiences relating to short-term missions are usually a result of poorly designed trips, misguided motives, or the immaturity of the participants. But let's not give up on short-term trips just because they are sometimes done badly. We must remember all of the ways short-term missions can make a positive impact when carried out in relationship to long-term strategies and priorities. The benefit comes from the synergy. When short-term experiences go badly, it is almost always because they have become disconnected from a long-term mindset. The danger comes from that disconnect, not the abbreviated time-frame.

Check-Box Mentality. When a short-term trip becomes disconnected from long-term missions, we may believe we have "done our bit" for missions and are now excused from further involvement. If I go somewhere hot and poor for two weeks, then I can check missions off my list. That attitude diminishes the vast, global, multigenerational nature of the Great Commission. "Missions inoculation" is a real danger, where a small exposure to the field numbs our desire for fuller and richer participation. Our Lord's command to disciple the nations cannot be satisfied by a few weeks of effort, no matter how hot it was, how poor the people were, or what kind of food we had to eat. None of us is finished with missions until Jesus returns or calls us home.

False Expectations. Short-term trips, especially for groups, are usually planned and organized in advance. Visitors who do not maintain a long-term mindset may think they have a better understanding of field life than is realistic given that food, housing, transport, and translators were prearranged for them. They may be unaware of how much effort has been exerted on their behalf by both missionaries and local organizers. Such a trip can also give a false sense of optimism about how much they have accomplished in a short time with little training, language ability, or cultural understanding. A church might begin to wonder, *If our college students led a dozen people to Christ in Honduras over spring break, why have our long-term missionaries won only a handful of converts in Uzbekistan in five years?*

> **"I've found that most short-term missionaries have an overinflated sense of the good they can do and an under-developed understanding of their potential to harm."**
>
> ~ CHURCH LEADER ~

Muddled Priorities. Many of the benefits of short-term missions relate to the spiritual development of the traveler. Visits can also be of great help to missionaries and the local church, and some make a significant contribution to reaching the unreached, but perhaps most often the value is in changing those who go. That's a valid benefit, but we need to be realistic about the purpose of each trip. Let's not pretend that our high schoolers are filling an essential role by painting a school in a country that has many underemployed painters. It's okay to send a youth group on a trip where the main purpose is to expose them to God's heart for the lost and the needs of the world. But let's make sure that the teenagers, their donors, and the receiving missionaries all understand and support that goal.

When planning a trip, we need to consider the impact on

the sending church, the traveler, the missionary hosts, and the receiving community. One or two stakeholders may have the priority on any given trip, but all of them should be considered and consulted. That's part of approaching short-term missions with a long-term mindset. It's a matter of alignment.

> "It's not that churches say they don't need to send career workers anymore. It's just that they prioritize funding and support to places where the church members can go and participate."
>
> ~ MISSIONARY ~

Distraction Factor. For the hosting field workers, short-term trips can be a distraction from ministry to the unreached. Darren Carlson gave an illustration of how a trip can come across to the receiving missionaries and communities:

> Imagine a team from France calls your church and says they want to visit. They want to put on VBS (which you have done for years), but the material is in French. They have heard about how the U.S. church has struggled and want to help you fix it. They want to send 20 people, half of them youth. Only two of them speak English. They need a place to stay for free, with cheap food and warm showers if possible. During the trip half of the group's energy will be spent on resolving tension between team members. Two people will get sick. They'd like you to arrange some sightseeing for them on their free day. Do you want them to come?[12]

It's important for visitors to coordinate their timing and activities with their partners on the ground so that the trip blesses rather than exhausts them.

Our team in Indonesia hosted a lot of short-term trips because we saw them as a strategic part of our ministry. As the number of trips increased, we eventually designated one team member to focus her time on facilitating the short-termers' involvement. She developed patterns for managing the trips that maximized the benefit for the visitors and for the ministry. For us, it was worthwhile, but not every team can devote that much time and energy to hosting guests.

Short-term experiences are one of the tools that make global missions accessible to most Christians. Almost any believer can find a way to use their gifts and skills to contribute to the great missions endeavor in a hands-on way for a short time, perhaps without ever leaving home. Many Christians who will never have the opportunity to serve long term on the mission field have been blessed, challenged, and inspired by visits to missionaries they pray for, ministries they support, and people groups that are in need of cross-cultural gospel workers. And many are making a difference through digital skills and virtual communication. When done wisely, short-term missions is an important complement to—not a replacement for—an incarnational presence among the unreached.

THE BOTTOM LINE

In light of technological and transportation developments, it is important that we incorporate short-term missions as a strategy for carrying out the Great Commission. Even the author who argues that short-term missions doesn't technically exist confirms that "church resources should be invested in short-term trips as a way of supporting missionaries," although he does not endorse them "as a separate missions strategy."[13]

As in so many important missions discussions today, there is no need for binary thinking. We do not have to choose between short- and long-term missions. They don't have to compete with one another. Let's commit to doing short-term trips well, making sure we have a clear goal that meets needs on the field. Missions, even on a short-term basis, should always be for the glory of God and the good of the unreached, not solely for the benefit of the traveler. Let's work hard to minimize the strain on the time and resources of the receiving missionaries or ministry. And let's think long term, even about short-term missions, and make an impact both during our time on the field and in our church community at home when we return. It's not just a trip. It's one piece of a lifetime of investment in God's redemptive plan.

The big picture, the Great Commission, requires long-term worldwide discipleship. Missions is a lifelong adventure for every believer, whether or not we ever set foot on foreign soil. Short trips and virtual interactions are important tools that the global church now has for accomplishing that great mandate. A glimpse of the front lines should leave us more in awe of the scope of His redemptive plan, more informed about how He is working in a particular context, and more motivated to ensure that He receives the glory due Him from every people group on earth.

DISCUSSION QUESTIONS

1. What benefits of short-term missions have you seen from the trips you have been on or observed?

2. What problems or mistakes have you seen in relation to short-term mission trips?

3. How does a long-term, big-picture mindset about missions inform your perspective about short-term missions?

4. How could you make a significant contribution to world missions through a short-term trip or virtual experience?

6

MISSIONARIES ARE HOLY, RARE, AND STRANGE

It has been said that Jesus promised his disciples three things—
that they would be completely fearless,
absurdly happy and in constant trouble.

—WILLIAM BARCLAY

Perception 6: Missions is only for eccentrics. Missionaries are either misfits in their home context or are "super-Christians" with an otherworldly call.

Our English word *eccentric* comes from the Greek terms *ek* (out of) and *kentron* (center). God's people have always seemed "off center" to a watching world. Like spiritual versions of Copernicus, they argue that earthly activities orbit around the Son, not the other way around. Christians who place God's purposes at the center of their lives, and their own interests at the periphery, seem odd indeed, yet it's through these eccentrics that God delights to reveal His glory and change the world.

Beyond the general eccentricity of all committed Christians, a subset of people often seems particularly odd even within the church—our missionaries. They really don't make sense at first glance. Why would someone jeopardize their career, leave loved ones, and risk their health and safety for an elusive task in a distant land?

> "There is an immediate other-ing of missionaries."
>
> ~ MISSIONARY~

I work with a lot of missionaries, and they are, truly, an unusual bunch. Today's missionaries, however, may not be quite as exotic as we imagine. Many of us picture middle-aged white couples in safari outfits and pith helmets holding a rifle or a piece of mystery fruit and frowning into the camera. That's not what missionaries are like now.

Today's missionaries come from all over the world. You can find them in the cockpits of major airlines, the lecture halls of top universities, and the conference rooms of urban high-rises. Some missionaries are Bible teachers, translators, and evangelists. Others are engineers, doctors, farmers, technologists, and entrepreneurs. Many have had professional careers, and some continue those careers on the mission field. Missionaries are also no longer as disconnected from their sending countries as they used to be. Many return home every home every year or two for brief visits. They can stay up-to-date on the latest sports scores, technology, cultural trends, and fashion. Some aspects of traditional missionary life have even gone mainstream. Many "normal" Westerners now travel internationally, sample exotic foods, and homeschool their children. And yet, the perception that missionaries are somehow otherworldly still lingers.

"Missionaries are holy, rare, and strange" was one of just

three perceptions on my survey that scored above average for both prevalence and impact. More than 80 percent of respondents marked the idea of missionaries being either oddballs or super-saints as "quite common," and another 8 percent identified it as "almost universal." Almost 90 percent said that it has at least some impact on missions engagement within the North American church. Field missionaries rated this perception higher on prevalence than church leaders, church members, or sending agency staff.

So what does that mean for missions? I have argued that missionaries fill a unique role in the church's Great Commission efforts and pushed back on the idea that every believer is a missionary. Does that mean that missionaries are a completely different category of Christians? Do they have a distinct calling that makes them unrelatable? And if they are no longer as strange as they used to be, are they still extra holy?

GOD'S MISFITS

Missionaries may not be as novel or socially out-of-step as they once were, but there will always be a distinctiveness about them. God has a habit of selecting unlikely people for His work. He empowers "the foolish things of the world to shame the wise . . . the weak things of the world to shame the strong . . . the lowly things of this world and the despised things . . . so that no one may boast before him" (1 Cor. 1:27–29). How normal do you think Noah was, spending years building a gargantuan boat

> "Sure, it's a calling, but we think we are fairly normal and kind of cool."
>
> ~ MISSIONARY~

while his neighbors scoffed and the local HOA sent him violation notices? God's choice of David, the least likely of his siblings, surprised even Samuel. Old Testament prophets include a colorful array of characters like Jonah, God's recalcitrant emissary to Assyria. Peter, a brash Galilean fisherman, and Saul of Tarsus, an academically elite enemy of all things Christian, both became pillars of the church. God has made many eccentric people, and He calls some of them to do special tasks for His glory. One of those special tasks is being a missionary.

> **"I don't think there is much wrong with a little weirdness in our missionaries."**
>
> ~ CHURCH LEADER ~

Years ago I had a breakfast meeting with the elders of a dynamic, growing US church. They had sent two women to outreach to a Muslin people group, so I took the opportunity to meet them while passing through the area. The group of high-powered men were full of vision and "go get 'em" American confidence. At some point between bagels and coffee refills they voiced some misgiving about whether they should have sent the single women as missionaries. They didn't use these exact words, but their question was essentially, "Shouldn't we be sending high-capacity, elder-qualified people like ourselves instead?"

I like to think that I responded diplomatically in the moment, but the thought going through my mind was, *Those women are exactly the kind of people you need to be sending. You would crash and burn in no time, and probably do a lot of damage in the process.* The aggressive cultural posture of the church leaders would not go over well among the high-context, relationally sensitive people group our team served. The women they had sent, however, were much loved and doing an amazing job. We don't just need to send good people to the mission field. We have to also send the right people. Not every effective church leader would make an effective missionary (and vice versa).

God has a mysterious selection process, but missionary service by its very nature often appeals to people who march to the beat of a different drum. "Normal" is defined by the majority, and the majority of Christians have little interest in moving around the world to evangelize people they've never met in places they've never been. Following the American Dream seems to make more sense. Missionaries tend to have a different frame of reference.

Arlene and I headed to the mission field for the first time when we were in our early twenties. Before departing, we visited a church to mobilize more workers and raise some financial support. A young couple was assigned to host us for lunch after the service and we enjoyed a pleasant afternoon at their home. All these years later, however, I distinctly remember the sense that we were living in different worlds. They were looking forward to promotions and home improvement projects. Arlene and I were packing four suitcases for departure to Indonesia, where I had secured a two-hundred-dollar monthly scholarship to study at a state university. They were great people, but we struggled to find common ground. Arlene and I hadn't yet left US soil, but that visit already felt like a cross-cultural experience.

In 1932 a British parlor maid named Gladys Aylward was majorly out of sync with the status quo. At twenty-eight, she was considered too old to become a missionary. She applied to a mission board and was turned down after a trial period because she lacked academic acumen, possibly due to a learning disability. Determined to reach China, Gladys saved enough money for a ticket on the Trans-Siberian railway and traveled alone through a war zone. Over the next seventeen years she became a Chinese citizen, advocated for the end of foot-binding, and cared for more than a hundred children through the horrors of the Second Sino-Japanese War. Reflecting on her remarkable journey, she famously observed, "I wasn't God's first choice for what I've done in China. . . . I don't know who it was . . . it must have been a man . . . a well-educated man. I don't know what happened. Perhaps he died. Perhaps he wasn't willing. . . . And God looked down . . . and saw Gladys Aylward."[1]

God calls unique people, and the role attracts some interesting personalities, but there are also environmental factors that add to the strangeness. Even if a particular missionary was only a little bit strange to start with, after they've spent a few decades living with nomadic sheepherders in Mongolia or motorboating up and down the Amazon, they aren't going to fit in very well back in Topeka. They've been assimilated to some degree into a different culture, language, economy, and value system. Their homeland has also changed while they've been away. Missionaries can never truly "go home" again. We should expect some strangeness from the people God has designated to carry His message to the least-accessible peoples of the world. It comes with the territory.

SPECIAL LIKE EVERYONE ELSE

So, granted, even modern missionaries can be a little strange, as they should be, but are they extra holy? More specifically, are they holier than an "average" Christian? In one specific sense, I certainly hope so. If you are the international ambassador of a king, you'd better know his intentions and represent him well. To fulfill the Great Commission, the church needs to send out gifted and motivated people to cross the language and culture barriers that separate people groups from the gospel.

Long-term cross-cultural missions is not for the faint of heart, and it's not for everyone. I hope we send emotionally and spiritually mature people who have immersed themselves in the Word, who are diligent in prayer, who are receptive to correction, and who serve others joyfully. Such qualities are essential for missionaries, but they aren't unique to missionaries. All believers should be growing in Christlikeness and personal holiness.

> "The common intensity of the missionary for the lost world often makes people feel somewhat spiritually inferior for not sharing it. They typically do not gravitate to conversations and relationships that make them feel that way."
>
> ~ MISSIONARY ~

As missionaries are sent out into the cross-cultural ministry arena, they will face many tough situations that will either make or break them. Hopefully they will grow in their faith and spiritual maturity. The path of obedience and sacrifice is not only a responsibility, but also a blessing. The arduous journey can accelerate a missionary's growth in holiness.

The people God chooses, and the church sends, to proclaim the gospel to the unreached are "extra holy" in the sense that they have been set apart for a specific, God-ordained task. Missionaries dedicate a portion of their lives to being witnesses in places and peoples and languages that are not their own. There's something sacred about it. Scripture admonishes us to honor those who lead the church and it is legitimate to have a similar attitude toward those who serve the unreached on behalf of the church.

In other areas of life, we naturally recognize and honor

people who are specialists in certain areas (doctors, musicians, athletes, scientists, firemen, artists, etc.) without adopting the unhelpful corollary that the rest of us are relegated to second-class status. We can all be patriotic, but that doesn't make everyone a soldier. We can celebrate the important role of a missionary without implying it is the only role that matters. God loves His children equally and every Great Commission role has dignity. Faithfulness takes many forms.

EARTHEN VESSELS

Emphasizing the need for spiritually mature missionaries does not imply they are immune from the struggles that every other Christian faces. Even fruitful cross-cultural servants have bad days, bad moods, and bad habits. That's another reason why missions is so challenging. God is using imperfect vessels—people who are still in process. The stress of a cross-cultural assignment can surface all kinds of issues that may have lain dormant in the relative stability of life in familiar and predictable surroundings. If this happens on short-term trips (and it does!) how much more so on long-term teams where missionaries can feel stuck and there's no end in sight?

> "I sense a seed of fear that prevents Christians from acknowledging missions as their own responsibility. They fear they will fail and so they leave it up to someone else. They miss their greater purpose and give up the wonderful opportunity of joining His work around the world."
>
> ~ MISSIONARY ~

Missions is not always a pretty picture. Tensions, conflicts, and sinful behavior happen all the time in day-to-day life at home and in our churches, but sometimes we are surprised when they also happen on the field. Even missionary giants like Paul and Barnabas argued and parted ways (Acts 15:39–40). It's not only surprising *who* God chooses to use, but also how much more

> **"I think the view of the missionary as oddball super-saint used to be more widely held but has decreased as personal brokenness has risen among people who go to the field."**
>
> ~ MISSIONARY~

work He wants to do in the life of each person He calls. Missions history has many forgotten casualties, including missionaries who crumbled, strayed, or despaired. May their stories remind us to encourage and support present-day missionary heroes in every way we can.

RARE BIRDS

If missionaries are often strange in the sense that they can lose touch with their own culture and if they are holy in the sense that they are set apart for a special type of service to God, then it stands to reason missionaries are also rare. Jesus Himself made this observation as He viewed the crowds: "The harvest is plentiful but the workers are few" (Matt. 9:37). Among unreached people groups around the world, it's easy to feel overwhelmed as an ambassador of the gospel. I remember visiting an island where eighty thousand people lived and there was no sign of Christian exposure—no crosses on calendars or gravestones, not a single Bible or believer or church. Faithful laborers in some parts of the world are few and very far between. While every follower of Jesus has been invited and commanded to participate in the making of disciples from every people group on earth, missionaries make up a much smaller subcategory of missions-minded believers. They will always be a minority in the body of Christ.

THE CALL

The concept of a "missionary call" adds to the aura of mystery surrounding global missions. If you are interested in becoming a missionary, how do you know if it's really God's leading or just your own altruism and sense of adventure? Given the sobering prospects of missionary work, should we wait for a voice from heaven? Some people move too fast without adequately seeking God, as Joshua did when he sampled the Gibeonites' moldy bread and then made a hasty treaty with them (Josh. 9:14–15). Others seem content to wait indefinitely for a bolt of lightning from heaven instead of pursuing what God has already made clear. There are times to wait, and times to step out by faith. Wisdom is knowing the difference.

> "Most believers don't personally know a missionary well. This makes for wrong thinking in the church that somehow going is an anomaly: 'It must be a little odd or strange if I don't know someone who's doing it.'"
>
> ~ MISSIONARY ~

The line between divine calling and wise decision-making can feel quite blurry. Does God have to call me into cross-cultural ministry to a specific people group? Or can I learn about the world and prayerfully choose a place I think I can make a difference? Some Christians believe that God gives specific instructions at a detailed level, while others say that we are free to choose within the boundaries God has provided. What some people label as "calling," others would describe as "commitment." Despite the confusion and differences of opinion, one thing is clear: the Great Commission is for the entire church. It does not include any exception clauses. If your view of calling exempts you from meaningful participation in God's redemptive plan, then you've already wandered away from His revealed will.

The Bible does not indicate that we must wait for a specific call before getting involved in missions. God defies our formulas. He has worked in different ways at different times. In Acts 13, at a formative stage of church history, the Holy Spirit specifically designated Paul and Barnabas for missionary service. We have little indication of similarly definitive divine selection of Paul's other companions. In Acts 16:9–10, Paul has a vision that he interprets as a direct call from God to go to Macedonia. At other points in his journeys, it appears that he made decisions based on his own strategic instincts, available transport, persecution, personal relationships, and many other considerations (Acts 13:50–51; 16:13; 18:1–3; 19:1, 21; 20:16; 21:2–3).

> "Our churches agree that missions is important, but most people in the congregations want someone else to do it."
>
> ~ MISSIONARY~

Evaluating all of the perspectives and implications on calling is beyond the scope of this book, but here are a few suggestions as you ponder how to make your best contribution in the global harvest:

Pray: Ask God to transform your heart and align your motives with His priorities. I frequently pray, "Lord, take away ideas and desires that are not from You and replace them with Yours," or echo the powerful heart cry of Psalm 67, "Lord, bless the nations through me."

Learn: Gather information about the aspects of missions that are new to you from books, online resources, and knowledgeable people. Research the needs of the unreached and what is being done to reach them. You can't respond to what you don't know.

Reflect: Take time to meditate on what you are learning in this season of life. Often our busyness gets in the way of hearing from God.

Dream: What might be your best contribution to the Great Commission? Let yourself think outside the box. Be creative.

Align: What practical steps can you take to align yourself more fully with the plan of God as you currently understand it? What would honor the Lord?

Trust: Fear keeps us in bondage, but "perfect love drives out fear" (1 John 4:18). As you delight in God, trust that He will guide you and take care of you.

Consult: God has placed us within the body of Christ. There is wisdom in the counsel of godly people (Prov. 24:6). Honor and trust the church leaders and mentors God has placed in your life.

Move: Take the next steps as you see them, even if they feel tentative. It's easier to steer a moving ship. Keep learning, reflecting, talking, engaging, and asking questions. You will shift course as God refines your understanding.

Rest: God stirs and unsettles us, but He is also the God of peace. Expect and pray that He will give you a sense of peace about the direction you are to go, even if it feels surprising, risky, or costly.

When we stray beyond biblical guidelines for making major decisions, we can get ourselves into (well-meaning) trouble. We can either be immobilized by indecision or race forward foolishly and presumptuously. If things go badly, we may easily fall into disappointment or cynicism. The key to good decision-making is to maintain a heart that is truly humble and teachable before God. We can follow the example of faithful Christians throughout the millennia who took simple, prayerful steps of obedience to God's written Word and therefore accomplished much for His glory.

IMPLICATIONS

We have explored some reasons why we may legitimately find missionaries to be strange. The danger comes if we extrapolate from there to say, "I don't find the missionaries I know attractive or relatable, so missions in general must also be unattractive and unrelatable." We may feel we aren't cut out to be evangelists in jungles or deserts, thinking, "If God meant for me to be a missionary, then it wouldn't seem so bizarre, I'd know exactly where to go, and I wouldn't be afraid of spiders." Maybe we can barely order at a French restaurant let alone learn an unwritten language. Maybe we don't look good in a pith helmet and can't face the prospect of living off a diet of insects and pig fat. So we excuse ourselves from Great Commission responsibility and move on with our lives. Missions is just too strange.

> **"Missionaries are someone else, not us. A strange, holy, set-apart breed."**
>
> ~CHURCH MEMBER~

Alternatively, instead of seeing missionaries as misfits, we may conclude, "Missionaries have to be super-Christians. I'm not holy enough to qualify, so I'm out of the game." We may look at well-scrubbed families standing on church platforms or smiling from prayer cards on our refrigerators, listen to stories of miraculous healings and transformed lives, and conclude that we could never measure up. Only super-Christians need apply.

Feelings of superiority and inferiority and a general sense of unrelatability are all tactics of the enemy to distance us from those individuals who are fully devoted to global missions. Whether we conclude that we are too normal and well adjusted to be missionaries, or that we are not high enough on the sanctification scale to qualify, or perhaps that we just didn't "get the call," we can end up excusing ourselves from Great Commission responsibility to the detriment of our faith, the unreached, and the global church.

IT'S OKAY TO NOT BE A MISSIONARY

Does the universal nature of global missions mean that every Christian has to become a missionary? Definitely not. Not every

Christian has the training, personality, character, and skills to move to a new context, learn another language (or several), perform cultural analysis, contextualize the gospel, translate Scripture, or lay the theological foundations for a healthy, reproducing church. The career missionaries who take on those tasks are not necessarily more gifted, more godly, or more faithful than the many people who stay behind to send them, but hopefully they are more suited to the specifics of their roles. As a global church, we rightly delegate some frontline tasks to those best able to complete them, but we shouldn't check missions off our to-do list after we mail a support check or say a "God bless the missionaries" prayer and then go back to our regular lives.

Fulfilling the Great Commission doesn't depend on one type of person (who evangelizes in their sleep, enjoys mosquitoes, and feels no need for privacy). And it doesn't depend entirely on missionaries. Spreading God's blessing to all the peoples of the earth depends on every type of believer working together, and that is

> "Missionaries do seem to be put up on a pedestal more than pastors. This can be a barrier to true partnership."
>
> ~ MISSIONARY ~

something worth celebrating. No matter your age, background, nationality, experience, education, or gifting, if you follow Jesus, you are invited to participate in the redemption of the nations. Celebrate the freedom in that invitation. It is easier to get involved in missions today than at any other time in history. Let's take advantage of that access and prompt each other to use our skills, talents, and spiritual gifts to glorify Christ among the unreached, realizing that for some of us that will mean becoming missionaries, and for most of us it won't. If you aren't cut out for direct cross-cultural ministry among the unreached, join the hundreds of millions of Christians who have impacted the world in a supporting role over the last two millennia. Be a sender, a pray-er, a giver, and an encourager. We need you. And I promise you don't have to wear a pith helmet.

THE BOTTOM LINE

The more separation we create in our minds between those of us who work on the missionary front lines and those of us who stay home as senders, the more difficult it is to build the community of the body across distance and culture. If we picture missionaries as otherworldly super-Christians with an exclusive calling that has no relevance to our own lives, we miss out on opportunities to participate in God's greatest mission. If we imagine that missionaries are so holy and so tough as to be immune from weakness, fear, or common everyday sin, we place them on a pedestal from which they cannot come down and deny them our understanding, accountability, and encouragement.

Let's reject the notion that missions is only for the radical few. It's time for the whole body of Christ to be mobilized. Missions isn't just for misfits—it demands the full application of all the best ideas, motives, character, resources, talents, and gifting the global church has to offer. We have a huge task to accomplish that requires everything we have to give. One of my mentors observed, "Reaching an unreached people group is much harder than putting people on the moon." Despite the challenge, we don't have to be perfectly sanctified to get started. The church is made up of hundreds of millions of people, each one with unique gifts and foibles. We can learn and grow together on the journey.

If you haven't already, try to get to know some real live

missionaries well enough to dispel some of the mystery of their role. Even if they are among the few who still live in a jungle and send their children to school in an airplane, you might be surprised by how much you have in common. All Christ followers share a special bond in the Holy Spirit. There's an even richer depth of relationship among believers who organize our lives around God's global discipleship mandate, no matter where we live.

If you feel strangeness radiating from the missionaries you know, you might be experiencing a little bit of culture shock. Keep in mind that they probably are too. Missionaries are bridges between cultures. We're usually okay with foreigners being different because we expect it, but we don't always extend the same grace to people who are a hybrid of multiple cultures. If our missionaries are too strange for us, just imagine the challenge of relating to the people they work among. We're all going to spend eternity together and it will be a wonderful experience! Why not get some practice now?

> "We have churches that give us a hero's welcome when we come home and treat us like superstars. I always find this uncomfortable."
>
> ~ MISSIONARY ~

If you feel overwhelmed by the details and possibilities for missions involvement, stop for a moment and remember the big picture. The Great Commission is for all of Jesus' disciples. God created each of us on purpose and gave us interests, skills, experiences, and spiritual gifts that contribute toward proclaiming His glory among the nations. We all have a part to play, not just the professionals, or the super holy, or the losers, or the misfits, or whatever other label we might use as an excuse to opt out. God's redemptive intentions are clear in Scripture. Don't let anything, not even the search for a specific calling, distract you from the revealed will of God. Whether or not you will become a missionary or in what location you will serve may be unclear to you right now, but you still have missions radar. Put down the carrots and prayerfully plot your course by what you see. And take heart if you aspire to cross-cultural service: you don't have to be weird to be a missionary. It's a perk that comes with seniority. Give it time.

DISCUSSION QUESTIONS

1. When you hear the term "missionary," what kind of person comes to mind? How are they different from you?

2. Do people you know tend to think of missionaries more as misfits or super holy? What effect do you think this has on their perception of missions?

3. How do you think people's view of missionaries is changing over time?

4. How have the missionaries you know influenced your perspective on missions?

7

MISSIONS IS HARMFUL

We face a humanity that is too precious to neglect.
We know a remedy for the ills of the world too
wonderful to withhold.
We have a Christ who is too glorious to hide.
We have an adventure that is too thrilling to miss.

—G. P. HOWARD

Perception 7: The overall effect of cross-cultural missions has been to propagate Western values and foreign versions of Christianity at the expense of local cultures.

In the *Star Trek* science fiction series, Starfleet officers are bound by oath to avoid interfering with other civilizations during their adventures across the galaxy.[1] Starfleet General Order 1, known as the Prime Directive, states: "No starship may interfere with the normal development of any alien life or society."[2] Captain Picard was willing to watch the destruction of the planet Boraal II from natural causes rather than rescuing and relocating its inhabitants.[3] He accepted the Prime Directive as an absolute, explaining to a crew member after a difficult decision, "History has proved again and again that whenever mankind interferes with a less developed civilization, no matter how well-intentioned that interference may be, the results are invariably disastrous."[4]

Global missions is, indisputably, a violation of the Prime Directive. Missionaries deliberately seek to engage and influence the communities they serve, some of which are less technologically and economically developed than their homelands. Are the results invariably—or even commonly—disastrous?

Whereas missionaries once enjoyed some measure of public support, times have changed. When Jim Elliot and his companions were killed in the jungles of Ecuador in 1956, news outlets hailed them as heroes. *Life* magazine featured their sacrifice in a ten-page spread titled, "Go Ye and Preach the Gospel: Five Do and Die."[5] Just over sixty years later, Jonathan Chau was killed on North Sentinel Island while trying to reach an isolated tribe with the gospel. In response, the *New York Times* published an article titled, "American's Death Revives Evangelical Debate Over Extreme Missionary Work."[6] A BBC News article the following week asked, "John Allen Chau: Do Missionaries Help or Harm?"[7] The BBC story presents multiple perspectives on missionary work, including a widely shared Facebook post where a woman questions her experience on short-term mission trips:

Why did I assume that my faith was the right faith? Why did I assume that my presence was so precious that it would change their hearts and lives? Why did I assume that they were lost, living their beautiful content lives right where they were? Why did I assume their lives needed changing?

This is white supremacy. This is colonization. White people entering a foreign land under the guise of caring to turn people into followers of the white peoples' god and life. Do not pretend colonization doesn't happen anymore. It just lives under a new name: mission trip.[8]

As Christ followers, how are we to respond to such an accusation? Is missions really colonial white supremacy under a different guise?

DO NOT DISTURB

Chances are, you have heard people associate missions with a legacy of imperialism, exploitation, and perhaps even racism. Almost half (47 percent) of our survey respondents said that the perception that missions harms cultures "somewhat" or "very much" influences believers. Thirty-seven percent rated this idea as "quite common" or "almost universal" within the North American church. Of all the categories of respondents, church leaders gave this perception the highest score for prevalence, with field missionaries rating it significantly lower. Perhaps people don't tend to express this idea around missionaries as often as they do in other settings.

> "My home church, being seeker friendly, is reluctant to publicly mention international ministries for fear of alienating people who see missions as cultural genocide."
>
> ~ MISSIONARY~

We hear a drumbeat of assertions by anthropologists, podcasters, TV personalities, and university professors that missionaries are the vanguard of cultural imperialism and have done irreparable damage to cultures around the world. For followers of Jesus, the idea that we might be destroying cultures should give us pause. It's a weighty charge. Have we really spent centuries coercing people into a Western value system at the expense of their cultures and traditions? As pursuers of truth, we want to acknowledge and correct anything that is hurtful or wrong. Our passion is to honor God and be good stewards of the world He created, including the beauty and diversity of human cultures. Christians should be protectors and guardians—not saboteurs—of all that is good.

> "The concept of missions as colonialism has been taught in the North American educational system and is almost universally accepted as fact by believers as well as unbelievers."
>
> ~ MISSIONARY ~

This issue hits home for me personally as well. I grew up in Papua, Indonesia, among a tribal people. My parents brought the gospel to the Sawi in the early 1960s. In many ways, our family represented the stereotypical foreign missionaries arriving in a previously isolated Stone Age tribe and introducing new information, technology, and values. It wasn't long before the Sawi abandoned their traditional soaring treehouses in favor of more permanent homes closer to the ground, just high enough to avoid the rainy season floods. They began using imported fishhooks, razor blades, knives, and matches instead of natural materials found in their environment. They donned Western clothes, carried water in tin cans instead of bamboo canisters, and hollowed out their long canoes with steel axes instead of stone adzes. Did my parents destroy Sawi culture? Would the Sawi be better off today if they had left well enough alone?

WHAT'S BEHIND THE PRIME DIRECTIVE?

Interestingly, *Star Trek*'s Prime Directive didn't materialize in a vacuum. The show first aired in 1966 during the middle of the Vietnam War. The Directive reflected a growing political sentiment that the United States should not interfere in the natural development of other countries. Ideas always have a context, and the notion that missionaries harm cultures is no exception.

Christ inaugurated His kingdom within human history and a sinful world. By its very nature this kingdom is a "resistance movement." It's a counterculture wherever it takes root, whether in the Roman Empire, Reformation-era Europe, Communist China, or the islands of the Pacific. And the reality is, though God's people are new creations, we still reflect and interact with the brokenness of the world around us. Jesus pointed this out when He told the parable of the wheat and the tares (Matt. 13:24–29). God's harvest grows side by side with weeds sown by His adversary. It takes a discerning eye to distinguish the two.

The modern chapters of Protestant missions, beginning around the time of William Carey and his contemporaries in the late 1700s, unfolded in the context of many such "weeds." European powers ruled the waves and partitioned the world. Looking back, it's not surprising that Christianity and missions are often identified with the excesses and abuses of the colonial era and more broadly with modern American and Western culture.

The awakening of the church to missions during the colonial era and the relationship of missions to geopolitical and sociological currents creates a complex picture. With growing access to the Scriptures, a renewed awareness of New Testament spirituality, a rediscovery of the Great Commission, and an increased exposure to the world and its needs, missionaries like Hudson Taylor and Jonathan Goforth began launching out to the "uttermost parts." They were aided in many cases by the access, resources, and protection afforded by European powers. At the same time, colonial authorities often obstructed missionary work. Those in power did not usually share the missionaries' enthusiasm for educating the local workforce, improving their welfare, or conferring the benefits of the Christian gospel. Contrary to the conventional narrative, the agenda of colonial-era missionaries was very often at odds with imperial interests, just as it is today.

During the age of colonial expansion, Christianity was often confused with "Christendom," and the gospel itself with the trappings of European civilization. The language and venues of the church were often leveraged to advance economic and national agendas and at times to justify exploitation and slavery. In 1492 Christopher Columbus landed on the island of Hispaniola, having promised a rich reward to the monarchs who funded his journey. Three years later he captured hundreds of Arawak tribespeople and sent them to Spain to be sold into slavery (most of whom didn't survive the trip). He wrote, "Let us in the name of the Holy Trinity go on sending all the slaves that can be sold."[9]

Without doubt, missionaries have sometimes fueled negative stereotypes. Some dishonored the name of Christ by prioritizing their own agendas, constructing fiefdoms, or abusing people they should have been serving. Others have ignorantly, arrogantly, or lazily replicated foreign forms of worship rather than doing the hard work of pursuing a contextualized, indigenous church. All over the world you can find Western-style church buildings, steeples, and robes in places they don't seem to belong. As the church globalizes and best practices are taught in mission circles, thankfully such patterns are becoming increasingly rare. Most missionaries now intentionally seek to communicate the gospel in ways that align with the honorable aspects of their host cultures.

A GALAXY OF DUBIOUS ASSUMPTIONS

Prime Directive or not, Starfleet crews were constantly interfering with the development of other civilizations. It would have been a very boring TV show otherwise. Captain Picard himself, despite his supposed adherence to the Prime Directive, once deliberately broke Edo law to save a single Federation citizen.[10] And not everyone bought into the Prime Directive, even in theory. When Spock first joined the *Enterprise*, he asked the first officer,

> "I find this view most prevalent outside of the church, although it may be an underlying factor as to why churches are not 'loud and proud' about their missions involvement."
>
> ~ MISSIONARY ~

"Have you ever considered that the Prime Directive is not only not ethical, but also illogical, and perhaps morally indefensible?"[11] That's a good question, Mr. Spock.

The claim that missionaries damage culture is growing, but it is not new. A 1982 *Time* magazine story on the impact of missionaries concluded, "It is difficult not to admire the zeal of . . . missionaries who have dedicated their lives to the selfless yet ultimately self-fulfilling task of spreading Christ's word throughout the world. Nonetheless . . . questions remain as to whether the spiritual good they do is not balanced, in part, by social and cultural harm."[12]

Today, an anti-missionary version of the Prime Directive is firmly lodged in the minds of many North Americans, if not consciously, then at least subliminally. Before we grow too embarrassed of our missionary predecessors, let's consider the facts carefully. As King Solomon noted, "In a lawsuit the first to speak seems right, until someone comes forward and cross-examines" (Prov. 18:17). Is it possible that the assumptions underlying the idea that missions has been—and still is—predominantly destructive are not as robust as they may first appear? Could these assumptions be "not only not ethical, but also illogical"?

The Bible doesn't matter. Claiming "missionaries mustn't tamper with other cultures" implies that what the Bible says is irrelevant. Just disregard the Great Commission. People don't need to be "saved" because there is no heaven and hell, only myth and superstition. The gospel is not actually good news. For committed Christians, this is the first and most fundamental consideration. Furthermore, because Bible-believing Christians are naïve followers of fanciful ideas, their motives and judgment are generally suspect. If they're gullible enough to believe a Jewish peasant is divine and rose from the dead, then they're probably wrong about a lot of other things too.

> "This perspective is more common in nominal believers and nonbelievers who have an overarching discomfort with someone claiming to have the truth."
>
> ~ MISSIONARY ~

But if the Bible is true and relevant, then we must obey it, and the Bible clearly tells us to "go into all the world" and influence other cultures (Mark 16:15). If God created the world and redeemed humanity, then His authority supersedes all cultures, and He has the right to command His church to spread His message and His glory.

All cultures, religions, and worldviews are equally valid.
"Don't interfere with the natives" rests on the assumption that all cultures are inherently good. Some people further believe that because culture is a system, to reject any part of it is to reject the entire integrated way of life. But pause for a moment. Do we really believe this? Does a culture really come as a package deal, or can some elements be unhealthy while others are wholesome or neutral? Can we really not discern the difference between positive and destructive cultural elements? Cultures exist today whose language, music, and dance are unique and beautiful, but who teach that twins are evil spirits and therefore must be killed at birth to protect the community.[13] Are we fine with a society that believes the antidote to a sore throat is bloodletting? Infanticide, widow-burning, female genital mutilation, and cannibalism are all ancient cultural practices. Do we really believe they should be preserved?

The Sawi people among whom I was raised were both headhunters and cannibals. They also considered an unconscious person to already be dead. It was a core part of their spirit-based religious worldview, not just a result of medical ignorance. If a man lost consciousness after being injured in battle, they would wrap him in a grass mat and place him in a small burial house on stilts. Sometimes the burial platform would shake for days as the victim struggled, drifting in and out of consciousness, before eventually succumbing to his injuries or dehydration.[14] Is it really wrong to interfere with such a tradition? After all, the goal of global health, economic, and agricultural programs is to change people's way of perceiving and behaving, which is to change their culture. The more I think about it, the more I agree with Spock. The Prime Directive is neither logical nor ethical.

Isolated people live in a utopia until missionaries arrive.
The stereotype of the "noble savage," uncorrupted by the evils of
civilization, featured regularly in European literature from the
fifteen to the nineteenth centuries and later in Hollywood movies.
The sad reality is that isolated peoples are not all living in bliss,
grass skirts rustling in the wind as they sip fresh coconut milk
beneath a palm tree. Whether remote or otherwise, all cultures
are afflicted with disease, corruption, poverty, illiteracy, sex traf-
ficking, wars, political and religious persecution, and a host of
other ills.

Our goal should be to preserve cultures exactly as they are.
The idea that missionaries destroy cultures by changing them implies that some cultures should be preserved without foreign influence while others are free to pursue rapid change. It's a double
standard that treats isolated cultures like specimens in a petri dish
rather than as human beings who share equal dignity, value, and
potential with us. I highly doubt whether putting a people group
in a cultural deep freeze is even possible, much less advisable, in
today's interconnected world.

Or is it only Christian missionaries who should keep their
distance, not secular influences? This line of thinking opens
another can of worms, since it's more often than not the missionary who loves the people, learns their language and culture,
and helps them survive the fast-approaching "Columbuses." My
father observed,

> There are reasons why the missionaries had to go into iso-
> lated areas like Irian Jaya as soon as they could. History has
> taught them that even the most isolated minority cultures
> must eventually be overwhelmed by the commercial and

political expansion of majority peoples. Naive academics in ivy-covered towers may protest that the world's remaining primitive cultures should be left undisturbed, but farmers, lumbermen, land speculators, miners, hunters, military leaders, road builders, art collectors, tourists, and drug peddlers aren't listening.

They are going in anyway. Often to destroy. Cheat. Exploit. Victimize. Corrupt. Taking, and giving little other than diseases for which primitives have no immunity or medicine. . . .

The question, "Should anyone go in?" is obsolete because obviously someone *will*.

It has been replaced by a more practical question: "Will the most sympathetic persons get there first?"[15]

While cultural preservation sounds noble, the truth is that cultures are always changing, with or without missionaries, and often change is for the better. UNESCO's World Commission on Culture and Development explains that "a society's culture is neither static nor unchanging but rather is in a constant state of flux, influencing and being influenced by other worldviews and expressive forms."[16] People love to advance and innovate and create. Trying to turn someone else's culture into a living fossil is neither realistic nor respectful.

We've no right to judge. Who decides which cultures should embrace change and which ones must be protected from change? Growing up in the jungle, I got to observe how secular "experts" interacted with missionaries and the local people. The occasional anthropologist or reporter would fly in on a missionary's airplane, eat his food, sleep in his home, and ask him lots of questions about the local culture since he spoke the language and knew the people. The outsider would then fly home and write an article about how missionaries are destroying cultures. Who is in the best position to critique a culture and evaluate the influence of missionaries on the local people?

The sixth century BC prophet Epimenides, later quoted by the apostle Paul, said of his own people, "Cretans are always liars, evil brutes, lazy gluttons" (Titus 1:12). Was it inappropriate for him to critique the behaviors of his own culture? Does not Western civilization progress (or regress) through a constant process of self-assessment? Paul urged Titus to try to change the toxic culture of Crete through sound teaching. He saw the gospel as God's instrument to break destructive cultural cycles.

> "I think this perception is uncommon, but those who hold to it are very vocal."
>
> ~ CHURCH LEADER ~

Even if we assume for a moment that only "insiders" have the right to judge their own culture, how can they be consulted without an outsider disturbing their isolation? And what if, given the choice, they prefer using matches to start fires, mosquito nets to reduce malarial deaths, and Vermox to rid themselves of intestinal parasites? What if they want to be free from the fear of evil spirits and generational cycles of revenge killings? What if they want a smartphone like yours? And watch out. They might politely suggest that our efforts to keep them in quarantine are little more than repackaged cultural imperialism.

Isolated peoples resent missionary influence. In my experience, tribal peoples around the world by and large love the missionaries who live among them and enjoy enduring personal bonds with them. It's the non-missionary outsiders they generally have trouble with—the traders, crocodile hunters, loggers, government officials, and sundry exploiters. The notion of the "ugly missionary" is, for the most part, a red herring.

One of the highlights of my missionary career has been the opportunity to attend several fifty-year anniversary celebrations of the gospel's arrival in jungle tribes. These multi-day convocations, full of joy and singing and dancing, are foretastes of heaven. Thousands of people gather in a jungle amphitheater. Festivities typically start with the oldest men and women retelling stories of how they used to live—the fear, bloodshed, wife-beating, and spirit worship. At some point the free-flowing program segues into fits of laughter as the missionaries' first arrival is reenacted, portraying their trunks of clothing, exotic food, linguistic blunders, and unorthodox ways. The humor eventually gives way to waves of worship, prayers of thanksgiving, unbridled dancing, and praise to the Lord for the life-transforming message of the gospel. This is not the reaction of an exploited people.

Missionaries spread a Western religion. We sometimes forget that Christianity is an Eastern religion. I hesitate to use the term "religion" with reference to the gospel, and it's not really "Eastern" because we know it is from God and not geographically constrained. Historically, however, Christianity originated in the Middle East before spreading to Europe, Africa, and Asia. Missionaries advocate for the beliefs and teachings of a four-thousand-year-old Middle Eastern nomadic tribe. Jesus and His Jewish disciples foisted their culture on the poor European barbarians! To be fair, their message of grace did a number on Jewish culture as well.

Many of the great church leaders of the first five centuries after Christ were from North Africa and Central Asia.[17] For generations after the resurrection, Christian missionaries were part of a persecuted minority, not a dominant political power. Keep in mind, too, that Christianity isn't the only religion to start somewhere and spread to foreign lands. If we view Christianity as a sort of invasive species, we must say the same for Islam, Hinduism, Buddhism, and various other religious persuasions.

All missionaries have pretty much the same effect. Painting an entire occupation or category of people with the same broad brush is dangerous. "Watch out for the fundamentalists," we hear, or "I had a bad experience at church when I was a kid, so I'm not going back." The church has sent out tens of thousands of missionaries from many countries over many centuries. They aren't all the same. When I was a child, the Catholic priest working in a tribe next to us often paid workers with cheap cigarettes. Once men became addicted, they'd keep working for more. My parents, on the other hand, taught the Sawi to be honest, to not steal, to count and read, and to start their own businesses so they would be able to compete with the outsiders who were beginning to arrive. Let's be specific about which missionaries we accuse of imperialism and why.

Missions is mostly about isolated tribes. The contention that "missionaries destroy cultures" presupposes that they work primarily among animistic tribes who have few outside influences. In some parts of the world, such ministry remains a significant part of the missionary task. However, a growing number of missionaries today focus on Buddhist, Muslim, Hindu, and secular people groups. Pioneers has many missionaries in Europe and North America. Most of our workers serve in major cities. And missionaries are now coming from other countries to minister in the US. The concern that missionaries are destroying cultures feels rather antiquated in a globalized world.

The impact of missions has been mostly negative. As we have acknowledged, terrible things have been done in the name of missions, the church, and Christ Himself. However, those terrible things were not carried out by gospel-loving, Spirit-filled members of the body of Christ. Most of these injustices were carried out by governments, businesses, and unbelievers using religion as an alibi or cudgel. The groups and individuals who acted unjustly needed the gospel themselves. It's too bad there weren't more missionaries to reach them.

Contrary to popular opinion, the impact gospel-centered missionaries have had on the world is overwhelmingly positive by social, economic, and human rights standards, even without considering the eternal benefit for people who had little hope of ever knowing Jesus. During the colonial era, many missionaries sought to protect the people they served from violence and disease. David Livingstone, a Scottish missionary whose heart is buried under a *mvula* tree in present-day Zambia, actually supported colonialism in sub-Saharan Africa in the nineteenth century because he hoped that European influence would put a stop to intertribal warfare and a brutal slave trade.[18]

Sociologist Robert Woodberry has identified a robust statistical correlation between "conversionary Protestant" missionary activity and the democratization of a country. His conclusion:

Areas where Protestant missionaries had a significant presence in the past are on average more economically developed today, with comparatively better health, lower infant mortality, lower corruption, greater literacy, higher educational attainment (especially for women), and more robust membership in nongovernmental associations.[19]

This was not a popular finding. Even the head of Woodberry's dissertation committee warned him of the inevitable backlash: "to suggest that the missionary movement had this strong, positive influence on liberal democratization—you couldn't think of a more unbelievable and offensive story to tell a lot of secular academics."[20] But after years of extensive research, Woodberry nevertheless concluded, "Want a blossoming democracy today? The solution is simple—if you have a time machine: Send a 19th-century missionary."[21] While Jesus didn't tell us to go into all the world and make people literate, rich, and democratic, Woodberry's findings illustrate the overwhelmingly positive influence of missionaries.

Another often-overlooked effect of missionary influence has been the preservation of languages. Language is the breath of a culture, and so the death of a language almost always results in the loss of a way of life. MIT linguist Norvin Richards expressed the importance of the preservation of languages and cultures well: "There are jokes that are only funny in Maliseet, and there are stories that only make sense in Lardil, and there are songs that are only beautiful in Wôpanâak. . . . If we lose those languages, we lose little pieces of the beauty and richness of the world."[22]

In 2019, the United Nations warned, "Almost half the world's estimated 6,700 languages are in danger of disappearing."[23] Many minority languages are lost when younger generations are educated in national languages. Written languages have a much better chance of survival than exclusively oral ones and many small, unique languages have been preserved by Bible translation. In one remarkable case, the Wôpanâak language was brought back to life a hundred years after its last speakers died. The linguistic revival was based on the translation work of Puritan missionary John Eliot.

The first Bible published in colonial America was in the Wôpanâak language in 1663. As a result of Eliot's literacy efforts, the Wampanoag tribe left behind a collection of written documents when disease ravaged their population. In the 1990s, Jessie Little Doe Baird, a descendant of the tribe Eliot sought to reach, used those records to revive the Wôpanâak language as part of a linguistics program at the Massachusetts Institute of Technology. Her daughter is the first native Wôpanâak speaker in seven generations and six other Wampanoags have become fluent in the language.[24] Interestingly, one of Baird's Wampanoag ancestors publicly opposed missionary work in the eighteenth century.[25]

A DIVINE DIRECTIVE

God loves the cultures of our world far more than Starfleet Command or Captain Picard did. After all, He invented them. The diversity of human cultures brings Him great delight and glory. God commanded Noah and his descendants to multiply and fill the earth (Gen. 9:7). Obedience would have naturally led to diversification. Instead, they built a city, clustered in one place, and fought to remain monocultural. They didn't want to be "scattered over the face of the whole earth" (Gen. 11:4). God responded by confusing their languages, jump-starting the process He'd originally planned, and forcing them to disperse into many cultures. He always intended a rich, diverse interweaving of peoples, languages, and societies.

And don't expect to say goodbye to your cultural distinctives in the next life. The closing chapters of Revelation (Rev. 21:24, for example) indicate that there will still be nations, kings, and cultures after this era of life on earth ends. John could somehow tell just by looking at the crowd around the throne of God that they were from "every nation, tribe, people and language" (Rev. 7:9). We will all be perfect, but we won't all be the same.

Missions is the transfer of the gospel across cultures, and the gospel is, literally, "good news." If we believe that the death and resurrection of Jesus supplied the only way to be reconciled with God, we need not shy away from influencing people accordingly. The gospel is good news for all people in all cultures. Sadly, many have not yet had the chance to hear it. We've been given a directive from heaven to track down and engage every culture with a mind-blowing, lifesaving message: "God so loved the world" (John 3:16). Our quest for those who will respond will carry us across all manner of barriers.

A GRAND REUNION

Fifty years after my parents brought the gift of the gospel to the Sawi people, I returned to the village where I grew up along with my father and two brothers. Our homecoming was documented in a fifteen-minute video called "Never the Same: Celebrating 50 Years Since Peace Child," available on the Pioneers website and YouTube. As I mentioned at the beginning of this chapter, many changes were immediately noticeable. For one thing, they took more pictures of us than we took of them! But more importantly, I noticed how many children there were. Fifty years earlier, most children didn't survive past the age of five. Elderly people also used to be rare. Accidents, disease, and their culture of pervasive violence all contributed to the early death of most Sawi people. They were constantly at war with one another and with the surrounding tribes, murdering and cannibalizing their victims. As a child, I almost never saw a Sawi man or woman with gray hair. Now, coming "home" after so long, I was surprised to see joy radiating from the faces of healthy people of every age.

Another thing that impressed me was the beauty of their language, which I could still understand even though I hadn't spoken it in decades. Almost everyone understood the national language, Indonesian, but they preferred to use their own language whenever possible. The New Testament had been translated into Sawi and many worship songs had been composed. Church services helped preserve their mother tongue and culture. What a blessing it was to listen to their humor and wonderful way of expressing things! The thought occurred to me that God was enjoying it, too, and that He had fashioned this people group to bring Him glory in a special way, distinct from every other.

The Sawi women asked about my mother, whom they loved dearly. As a nurse, she had saved many of their lives and delivered their babies. They called her "the woman who makes everyone well." As they grieved to hear of her passing, I was reminded of how deep our relationships forged in the family of God can be, and the special joy of experiencing the bond of Christ across cultures.

And it wasn't just the Sawi who gathered. They invited four other tribes—former enemies and the victims of their brutal cannibal rituals—to celebrate with them. Some Kayagar men who had courageously brought our family to the Sawi village in their canoes fifty years earlier escorted us from the float plane to the shore. They symbolically lined their canoes with spears and arrows as a reminder that they had feared for their lives when they ventured into enemy territory the first time to deliver our family to this very spot. Now these tribes socialize, worship, and intermarry in peace. They don't bother to build homes high in the treetops anymore because they no longer live in terror of their neighbors. The gospel has broken through the resentments and cycles of vengeance that once divided and ravaged their communities. Together, the Five Tribes, as they call themselves, have formed an alliance committed to spreading the gospel message even farther afield.

Among the Sawi, as in so many places, missionaries came with all their fallibilities, default settings, and eccentricities. But they also came with a Helper, the Holy Spirit, and with a biblical compass and humble hearts. God used these imperfect vessels to establish yet another community of re-created people in yet one more language and culture, for His eternal glory. A Sawi friend from childhood, now a senior elder in the church, summed it up well: "We're going to stay faithful to the gospel as long as we live. It's everything to us."

THE BOTTOM LINE

The misperception that missionaries do more damage than good, as prevalent as it may be, should not discourage us from pressing onward with the task God has given us. The reality is, missions is a lifeline for people and cultures all over the world. Our missionary calling rests on theological foundations—the lostness of man, the provision of God, and the privilege of stewardship. God created us, He sees the big picture, and He's given us a message of hope to convey to the peoples of the world. If we have a genuine concern for other cultures, obeying the Great Commission is the most loving thing we can do. Our main question should no longer be, "Is missions worth doing?" but, "Are we doing justice to this radically God-glorifying, lifesaving message that has been entrusted to us?"

Answering the accusation that missions is harmful requires accurate definitions, a more complete understanding of circumstances, and an examination of assumptions. We must distinguish between the core task of global missions and the faulty and ethnocentric ways it has sometimes been carried out. The church and the messengers aren't perfect, yet God has chosen to work through us. Plenty of people have fallen short in the course of history, whether with true motives or false. That reality

> **"The idea of perfection deters us all, especially Westerners. We need to tweak our methodologies and learn, but we can't be effective if we live under this pressure that we have to do everything perfectly before we can begin."**
>
> ~ CHURCH LEADER ~

mustn't trick us into unwittingly joining their ranks by shirking our own responsibility. The fact that we do missions imperfectly should not prevent us from attempting it at all.

If the world is not supportive of our missionary efforts, we should be neither surprised nor discouraged. Jesus warned that we would encounter skeptics (John 15:18–20). Missionaries are best friends to people and cultures around the world to the extent that they are guided by the Holy Spirit and the love of God as revealed in His Word. They have been enthusiastic advocates for indigenous cultures—speaking their languages, treating the sick, caring for the needy, and assisting in their inevitable transition to modernity. The evidence of their impact is seen in the lives of hundreds of millions of faithful disciples of the Lord Jesus. Every Christian and every church in the world can ultimately be traced back to the work of missionaries.

In its pure form, missions is a supreme act of sacrifice, not selfishness or imperialism. It's an expression of incarnational ministry, reflecting what Jesus did in leaving heaven. He committed the ultimate violation of the Prime Directive when He incarnated in our human culture and sacrificed Himself for our salvation. Our responsibility is not to leave the planet undisturbed, but to redeem by the power of God what has been corrupted by sin, making way for peace, joy, and creative expression. God gave us the Great Commission precisely because He loves the peoples of the world too much to preserve them as they are.

DISCUSSION QUESTIONS

1. Does the word "missionary" carry any sense of embarrassment or stigma in your mind? If so, why do you think that is?

2. In what ways was Jesus a missionary? How did He relate to the culture around Him?

3. When do you think it might be appropriate to challenge or change someone else's culture?

4. What do you think of the idea that we'll still have distinct cultures in heaven?

8

MISSIONS IS FAILING

*So the vision of our world-sized part depends not
so much on who we are, why we're here, or where we're going.
Rather it depends on who Christ is, why He's here, and where
He's going—because we are following Him.*

— DAVID BRYANT

Perception 8: On the whole, missionaries haven't made much impact. As the world population grows, we may even be losing ground. Our strategies haven't worked well.

Børge Ousland and Mike Horn set out to cross the polar ice cap on skis on September 11, 2019.[1] Ousland had already skied to the North Pole twice before and Horn had kite-skied across Antarctica. Both men knew what they were doing, but neither anticipated what lay ahead. They skied in perpetual sunset for eleven days, then in uninterrupted darkness for more than two months, each pulling a sled loaded with 410 pounds of supplies.

Horn and Ousland's target pace was eleven miles per day, but for parts of the journey they struggled to make five. The fissures in the ice turned out to be wider and more numerous than expected and they had to paddle across open water in inflatable rafts, towing their supply sleds. Frostbite and infection rendered Horn's hands almost useless. But there was an even greater, unseen threat to their expedition: the ice was working against them.

There is no land at the North Pole. Ousland and Horn were crossing the Arctic Ocean on free-floating ice. They planned their trip so that the ocean currents would accelerate their progress, much like a moving walkway at an airport. They soon discovered, however, that the ice was so thin that it was being directed, not by the predictable currents, but by the wind. And the wind was blowing against them. Every time they stopped to rest, they drifted backward. On November 14, a storm blew them backward for twenty-eight miles. Each of the next three days they skied across the 86th parallel only to be blown back at night as they slept.

Have you ever felt like the ground was moving backward under your feet? I once climbed Mt. Semeru, the highest volcano in Java. The steep upper slopes consist of sand and loose gravel. With every step forward, I found myself sliding back down the mountain. Missions can feel like that sometimes. Tens of thousands of missionaries have been sent out, yet thousands of people groups remain unreached. As the church grows, so does the world's population. Unreached people are born every day. Does that mean the gospel is losing ground? Are our strategies really that flawed and our efforts really bearing so little fruit? How can we be sure whether the ice is drifting backward, or whether it is an optical (or statistical) illusion?

A TROUBLING PICTURE

The sobering reality of global missions is that there is still a massive amount of work to be done. The Joshua Project identifies

7,387 unreached people groups that make up 42 percent of the world's population.[2] Of those unreached groups, 4,996 are less than 0.1 percent Christian and have no viable, self-propagating gospel witness.[3] In September of 2021, the International Mission Board regarded 347 people groups (representing more than twelve million people) as having no local evangelical Christians or churches and no access to significant evangelical print or digital media resources. A further 4,770 people groups (over a billion people) were less than 2 percent evangelical and had little, if any, active church planting effort.[4] Wycliffe Bible Translators estimates that work on a Scripture translation for 1,800 languages has not even begun.[5]

> "I think a little more of this kind of perception among followers may be helpful in forcing people to rethink the same old strategies that we've been trying for decades. A lot of time and money is spent doing the same things that aren't working."
>
> ~ MISSIONARY~

Another discouraging dynamic is that Christianity seems to be retreating in certain parts of the world. In Iraq, for example, the Christian community has dwindled by 83 percent in less than twenty years, from around 1.5 million in 2003 to just 250,000 today. "Christianity in Iraq . . . one of the oldest Churches, if not the oldest Church in the world, is perilously close to extinction," the Archbishop of Irbil recently lamented. "Those of us who remain must be ready to face martyrdom."[6] According to the *World Christian Encyclopedia,*

> The most important case for the shrinking of Christianity is the North Africa-West Asia region, which includes Iraq, Syria, Israel, Palestine, and Turkey. This region has been

under enormous pressure in the 20th and 21st centuries and has experienced a precipitous drop in its Christian population, from 12.7 percent to 4.2 percent in 2020. Turkey in particular was 22 percent Christian in 1900 and is only 0.2 percent Christian today.[7]

These are not the kind of statistics I enjoy reading. It can appear, based on certain data, that we not only have a long way to go to fulfill the Great Commission, but may even be losing ground in some areas. The *World Christian Encyclopedia* summarizes the situation this way: "The percentage of the world that is Christian has changed very little over the last 120 years. In 1900, 34.5 percent of the world was Christian; in 2020, the figure is 32.3 percent."[8]

The idea that missions is failing seems to be common within the North American church. Of all the categories of survey respondents, church leaders were the most likely to rank it in their top three perceptions that are hindering the North American church's missions engagement. Church members gave it the highest scores, compared to other groups, in both prevalence and impact.

> "Who wants to support a sinking ship? It is hard to swim against that stream of opinion."
>
> ~ MISSIONARY ~

The perception of failure within the church may be unwittingly bolstered by advocates of new missions tools and strategies, who often begin by describing the inadequacies of the old ways. It's difficult to find a more discouraging summary of the current state of missions than the opening chapter of a book that claims to have discovered the solution. If only we had pursued the right strategy! The key has now finally been found—that is, until the next new idea pops up and repeats the cycle. Intentionally or not, this kind of thinking discourages God's people. Are we, as a global church, drifting backward on free-floating ice, driven by winds we didn't anticipate and don't understand?

FINDING SOLID GROUND

Before we sink into missiological despair, let's consider the possibility that the scale of the remaining work does not necessarily suggest sweeping failure. God is painting a picture that we don't fully grasp. We have only a limited view of the scope, time frame, and characters of God's masterpiece and our own place on the canvas. God is a God of surprises, and His plan involves twists and turns. At every point in history some local expressions of the church have been strong and others weak. In fact, missions has been an unlikely enterprise from the very beginning. Gordon Olson describes the situation of the disciples who originally received the Great Commission: "Their leader had been crucified like a common criminal; their treasurer had betrayed Him and committed suicide; their chief spokesman had denied that he had even known Him; and the rest were a sorry lot of scattered cowards."[9] It did not appear to be a winning formula, yet those eleven disciples changed the world.

Today, some congregations, denominations, and church networks are always suffering or dissolving while others thrive and multiply. Dr. Timothy Tennent, president of Asbury Theological Seminary, writes, "The largest churches in Western Europe are pastored by African Christians. The fastest growing churches in North America are the ethnic churches. Global Christianity is actually the greatest force for renewal in the North."[10] Take heart, the Father is faithfully preparing a spotless bride for His Son.

Regardless of what we may see in any particular context, God's global church is growing faster, both in terms of individual believers and diversity of people groups, than at any other point in history. *Operation World* estimates that the evangelical church includes 546 million people, or 7.9 percent of the world's population, and is growing at an annual rate of 2.6 percent.[11] That is more than double the growth rate of the global population (just over 1 percent in 2020).[12] The *World Christian Encyclopedia* states, "The number of Evangelicals in the world has increased from 112 million in 1970 to 386 million in 2020."[13] The IMB estimates that active church planting is underway in 2,100 unreached people groups.[14] Consider some highlights:

Africa: The evangelical church grew from 1.6 million in 1900 to 182 million in 2010.[15]

Latin America: The evangelical church grew from seven hundred thousand in 1900 to ninety-one million in 2010.[16]

Asia: Protestant, Independent, and Anglican Christians increased from three million in 1900 to two hundred million in 2010.[17]

Europe: Evangelicals are growing at an annual rate of 1.1 percent, matching the global population growth rate.[18]

The picture is equally as encouraging on a country level. In 1966, Nepal had five hundred known Christians. By 1998, the Nepali church had grown to over 200,000 believers.[19] In 2010, *Operation World* estimated Nepal was home to 838,000 evangelicals with an annual growth rate of 5.3 percent.[20] Between 1960 and 2010, Peruvian evangelicals increased forty-fold in the midst of "violence and social breakdown," despite 750 evangelical leaders being martyred and many others imprisoned.[21] Over the same fifty years, the evangelical church in Brazil grew from 2.9 percent of the population to 26.3 percent.[22] A *Forbes* article in 2016 estimated there were between 300,000 and 500,000 believers in North Korea despite decades of massive, sustained persecution.[23]

In the aftermath of Iran's 1979 revolution, evangelism was made illegal, missionaries were forced out, and Bibles in Persian and Farsi were banned. The country's five hundred believers were cut off from outside resources and support. Rather than withering away, the Iranian church flourished. In 2015 it was described as the fastest-growing evangelical church in the world, and Iranians were playing a significant role in reaching Afghans, who became the second-fastest-growing evangelical church that same year. The Gospel Coalition estimates that "more Iranians have become Christians in the last 20 years than in the previous 13 centuries put together since Islam came to Iran."[24]

> **"From the West it may seem missions is failing, but from the field, God is at work."**
>
> ~ MISSIONARY ~

Clearly, the Holy Spirit has done a mighty work through His church in the last century, and He isn't finished yet. The growth of the church is often hidden because God is on a stealth mission. He frequently works undercover, redeeming people and building His church quietly. God has an amazing ability to hide His work in plain sight. His kingdom grows slowly and inexorably, like a mustard seed.

In the late 1970s, I joined a prayer group every Wednesday before school to pray for the church in China. We had very little information about what was happening spiritually in China, but we prayed that God would do a mighty work. A few years later, when China reopened to the world, we were amazed to learn that the church had grown from one million believers in 1949 to at least four million in 1980, despite intense government persecution.[25] In 2021, the *World Christian Encyclopedia* described the church in China as fifty-six million strong.[26] Some estimates are much higher. For example, *Operation World* suggests the number is more than eighty million.[27] In our modern era we may think we know what's going on globally, but there is still much that we don't see. The day will come when God throws off the camouflage. Until then, we hope and trust in His plan, even though we feel the wind blowing against us.

The old expression "God has no grandchildren" carries more than a kernel of truth. Every generation must be re-evangelized and discipled. I've appreciated Philip Yancey's observation in this regard:

> God "moves"—in the most literal, change-of-location sense—in mysterious ways. To visit the burgeoning churches of the Apostle Paul's day, you would need to hire a Muslim guide or an archaeologist. Western Europe, site of the Holy Roman Empire and the Reformation, is now the least religious place on earth. . . .

> Meanwhile, the greatest numerical revival in history has occurred during the past half-century in China, one of the last officially atheistic states and one of the most oppressive. Go figure.[28]

God has explained His global redemption plan to us, but not its time frame or the specific mechanisms He will use to bring it about.

Another example of Great Commission progress that we do know about involves New Guinea, the second largest island in the world (after Greenland). New Guinea and the surrounding islands are home to one-fifth of the world's languages. Seventy years ago, few of New Guinea's 1,300 language groups had a church presence. To put some perspective on that number, if you said the name of one group every two seconds, it would take nearly an hour just to read the list of people groups that needed the gospel. Today, I'm not aware of any of these groups that don't have their own churches. How did it happen? Missionaries from about two dozen agencies have been hard at work for decades planting and watering the gospel seed in partnership with local believers. These thousands of churches can all be traced, without exception, to the diligent and coordinated missionary efforts of God's people.

In recent years there has been a great acceleration in reaching unengaged people groups. According to Finishing the Task, between 2005 and 2020, 3,158 people groups were engaged for the first time by 5,159 missionary teams.[29] We live in a truly remarkable age. Sending cross-cultural missionary workers to every one of the remaining people groups is achievable in our lifetime. The Lord of the harvest is redeeming His children from among all the nations, and we are making great progress in sending emissaries to every ethnic group on earth.

MANAGING EXPECTATIONS

When I first took a leadership role at the Pioneers mobilization base in the US, the leader of another mission agency called me up. "It's not going to be long before there won't be any more unreached people groups," he said. "What will Pioneers do then?" Maybe he was concerned that I would soon be out of a job! I reassured him, "I think that's probably a little farther off than you think. We'll gladly deal with that problem when the time comes." That was more than twenty years ago.

> "In the circles I've been in, people are usually shielded from this perception because they have been fed inflated statistics about the numbers of 'conversions,' 'baptisms,' and 'church plants' that their valuable donation has produced."
>
> ~ MISSIONARY ~

Sometimes, in our enthusiasm for global missions, we may overstate our Great Commission progress. It is difficult to keep the right blend of positivity and sobriety, striking a balance between celebrating what God has done and remembering how much work remains. Sometimes ministries are tempted to exaggerate their successes as they report to donors year after year. Sometimes ministries inadvertently duplicate their results. Several organizations may partner together and each report on the same events, giving the impression that more people have been baptized or more churches started than is actually the case. Sometimes we count new members enthusiastically, but don't include a column on the spreadsheet for those who stop coming. Perhaps at times we just believe we've had more of an impact than we really have. We want to measure the harvest to evaluate our impact, but in

God's design there can be seasons of ministry where the seed lies dormant. How long might we plant and water seeds in Saudi Arabia, for example, before we see an Iran-like harvest?

Our generation has access to a wealth of ethnographic information about the peoples of the world. Missions-minded Christians have built databases identifying whether each group has been engaged by a church planting team, if they have the *Jesus* film, if there are any known believers, how much Scripture they have in their language, and other important markers. Such tools are very helpful as we identify needs and send out workers. However, let's be realistic about how far along we really are.

For example, we rightly celebrate when churches adopt unreached people groups for focused prayer and involvement (we'd love to see more of this!), but that doesn't necessarily mean that anyone in that people group has heard the gospel yet. It's great cause for celebration when the *Jesus* film is made available in another language. Now, how can we ensure that people have access to it and are coming to faith in Christ as a result? And who is teaching the new believers all the things that Jesus commanded? These are all examples of encouraging mile markers on the way to a very challenging goal. Ultimately, the Great Commission is about making mature disciples. Let's be encouraged by each step forward but keep our eyes on the big picture.

The Bible is not against counting results—Acts often references the numerical and geographical growth of the church—but measuring Great Commission progress calls for care, integrity, prayer, and a long-term, biblical perspective. Discipleship can be arduous and difficult to quantify. Believers who have walked with the Lord for decades still need teaching and correction. How much more so fledgling churches in remote locations and hostile communities? Even the disciples felt Jesus was on the slow boat at times: "They gathered around him and asked him, 'Lord, are you at this time going to restore the kingdom to Israel?'" (Acts 1:6). They could hardly wait to "get the show on the road" and take their leadership seats in the new administration.

Each one of us is a very small piece of a very big puzzle. Let's not become heady when God uses us for His glory. Setia, one of the most effective national evangelists I know, only has one name. Western Union requires a last name for wire transfers, so my wife and I literally send funds each month to "Setia Noname." I love that. May we all be willing to serve in anonymity. As for our Great Commission expectations, world evangelization happens on God's timetable. Let's serve with a sense of heavenly urgency, but not worldly impatience. The wind may be against us, but we aren't drifting backward on free-floating ice. There is solid ground beneath our feet after all. Our mission is rooted in the authority and power of God.

WHEN FORWARD FEELS LIKE BACKWARD

One reason that Great Commission progress is not always obvious is because it's difficult to quantify such a complex endeavor. Cultures don't usually have clear borders, and neither do languages. India is an especially challenging environment because it encompasses so many castes and categories. Where does one group end and the next begin? How much must dialects and worldviews diverge before interactions between them become cross-cultural? Sometimes the first missionary to move to an unreached area discovers that what they thought was one people group is actually five communities with different dialects and somewhat unique subcultures. One step forward for world missions, four steps back on the unengaged people group list. It's progress that doesn't look like progress.

While precise definitions differ, most missiologists categorize a people group as *reached* when at least 2 percent of the population is known to be professing Christians. The theory is that this critical mass of believers will have the momentum to continue evangelizing and discipling the rest of their community. Only God knows the reality in any given context, but 2 percent is our best estimate of church planting critical mass.

Two percent is a small portion of a population, but for many ethnic groups, it's still a lot of people. For example, the Shaikh of Bangladesh, one of the largest unreached people groups in the world, number more than 125 million.[30] If a missionary to the Shaikh, blessed with Jonah-caliber effectiveness and a Nineveh-scale response, established a church of a hundred thousand believers, it would still represent less than a tenth of a percent of the population. To be designated "reached," 2.5 million Shaikh individuals have to embrace the gospel. From a human perspective, at least, it will likely take decades for such a large church community to form. The fact that the Shaikh and thousands of other people groups remain unreached does not mean that God is not at work or that missionaries are being ineffective. It simply means that we aren't finished.

As we mentioned earlier, there's no question that some former centers of the Christian faith are now mission fields once again. But that does not necessarily mean the church is shrinking overall. Part of the decline in the number of Christians in the Middle East and Central Asia is the result of many of those Christians fleeing persecution to safety in other countries. As with the Jerusalem church in Acts 8:4, "Those who had been scattered preached the word wherever they went." While their scattering may seem like a step backward, we can trust that it is part of God's strategy to spread the gospel.

INTERPRETING THE DATA

If it is so difficult to make sense of the data on global missions, how can we make good decisions about where to invest our lives and resources? For starters, it's helpful to distinguish between reports on the status of Christianity and the state of the church. When people say, "Christianity isn't growing," they are often re-ferring to what has often been called "Christendom" rather than to the actual body of Christ. Christendom is a fusion of political and religious identity. It's more of a sociocultural con-struct than a matter of saving faith. I'm not personally very interested in Christendom. I'm interested in the church—those who have professed faith in Christ and been born again by the work of the Holy Spirit. I care more about how many people groups have healthy, reproducing churches than how many countries' populations identify themselves largely as Christian. Our task is to establish mature disciples, not to convince people to mark "Christian" on a census.

"A balanced and truthful account of God's hand in global missions should be shared more often in all our churches, as the weight of all the sin and negativity in the news does quench the enthusiasm of the church."

~ CHURCH LEADER ~

Operation World estimated that in 2010 the growth rate of Christianity was around 1.2 percent, while the evangelical growth rate was 2.6 percent.[31] That's a big difference. The author explains that, for the purposes of statistical analysis, "the measure for theological orthodoxy in [*Operation World*] figures comes not with the label *Christian*, but with the label *evangelical*."[32] Definitions of evangelicalism differ somewhat, but usually include four basic criteria, quoted here from *Operation World*:

> The Lord Jesus Christ as the sole source of salvation through faith in Him, as validated by His crucifixion and resurrection.

> Personal faith and conversion with regeneration by the Holy Spirit.

> Recognition of the inspired Word of God as the ultimate basis and authority for faith and Christian living.

> Commitment to biblical witness, evangelism, and mission that brings others to faith in Christ.[33]

Only God knows who is truly "born from above," but when it comes to statistics on global church trends, the "evangelical" category is usually most relevant.

Careless mixing of categories can paint an unnecessarily gloomy picture. For example, the situation in Europe looks dour if we accept that it was once a Christian continent which has now lapsed into secularism. However, it is highly questionable whether parts of Europe were ever broadly evangelized in the first place. A wave of nominal Christians declaring themselves to be atheists does not mean that the true church is shrinking. Those unbelievers are no more lost now than they were before.

In some respects, they may actually be easier to distinguish and reach now.

DEFINING SUCCESS

Because the Great Commission task is so vast and so complex, God has given us more than one paradigm through which to view the harvest. Passages like Matthew 24:14 emphasize the *ethne*, a multicultural mandate: "This gospel of the kingdom will be preached in the whole world as a testimony to all nations, and then the end will come." Acts 1:8 presents a geographic lens: "You will be my witnesses in Jerusalem, and in all Judea and Samaria, and to the ends of the earth." The gospel must go everywhere. And 2 Peter 3:9 is an example of the individual mandate: God "is patient with you, not wanting anyone to perish, but everyone to come to repentance." Paul writes of a "full number of the Gentiles" who will be saved, indicating that God is keeping count (Rom. 11:25). Our sense of progress may depend on which lens we happen to be looking through. Are we most concerned with reaching every individual, every location, or every people group? God is looking at the entire integrated picture, and His timetable is perfect. I find that reassuring whenever I feel overwhelmed or anxious. God's great harvest will come in the "fullness of time," when Christ comes as the head of all things (Eph. 1:9–10 ESV). We just don't know when that is.

While some of us can become overwhelmed by the Great Commission, to others it doesn't actually sound that hard. If, as *Operation World* estimates, there were about 546 million evangelical Christians in the world in 2010, that makes seventy-three thousand evangelicals for every unreached people group.[34] It doesn't sound very hard to divide up the list and get to work. If every megachurch sent a team to an unengaged group, wouldn't we be done in a decade or so?

A retired Army colonel once visited our team in Indonesia with a similar sense of optimism. After learning about our work and touring the city, he suggested that we needed a new strategy for reaching the thirty-two million Muslims around us. Addressing our team of thirty missionaries at a dinner meeting, he proposed, "What you need to do is start leading people to Christ. If each of you brings one person to faith each week, and that person does the same, and so on, then you will have thriving churches here in no time." Why hadn't we thought of that?! If only it were so simple.

Western Christians' "can-do" spirit and our ability to "organize our way to success" are wonderful contributions to the global body of Christ, but our strengths have vulnerabilities and blind spots as well. Plans and formulas have their place, but how things play out in real life, even in the pages of Scripture, can be wonderfully unpredictable.

One of the most dramatic examples of God's unexpected methods occurred on the island of Java, Indonesia. A handful of faithful missionaries had been tilling the soil and sowing gospel seeds among Javanese Muslims with a small but growing number of churches to show for their efforts. In 1965, political turmoil and a government coup unleashed tremendous social upheaval in Indonesia. Thousands of people lost their lives in the chaos that followed. Suddenly, Christians were seen as sources of help and refuge for those fleeing their enemies, and many people came to faith in Christ. A book by Avery Willis documents two million Javanese from a nominal Muslim background being baptized in a period of six years.[35] Today, approximately 5 percent of the nearly one hundred million Javanese are Christians.[36] No missionary had "coup, social upheaval, and violence" listed on their strategic ministry plan for 1965, but through those events God multiplied the impact of His faithful servants who had been laying a foundation for decades in anticipation of a coming harvest. In His own time, God brought the abundant fruit.

When Jesus traveled through Samaria, one conversation with a woman at a well led to the salvation of many people in her village (John 4:39). Jesus challenged His disciples to open their eyes and consider the abundant spiritual harvest. He then explained, "I sent you to reap what you have not worked for. Others have done the hard work, and you have reaped the benefits of their labor" (John 4:38). Jesus implied that some kingdom work is harder and more foundational than other aspects. Over the centuries, faithful laborers have tilled the soil in difficult places, planting, weeding, and watering so that we can now celebrate a bountiful harvest. In other places, a new generation of missionaries is just now clearing the land.

Henry Blackaby's excellent book *Experiencing God* emphasizes that we should "watch to see where God is working and join Him."[37] There's a lot of truth to this, but also a hidden danger. If we only go where we see God currently working, what about the neglected places? What about the places where the Spirit of God wants to reap a harvest twenty or thirty years from now? Who will do the "hard work" in Saudi Arabia and Yemen and Mauritania in anticipation of a future God-glorifying harvest that seems impossible now?

God has not limited our task to the places where fruit is already falling off the tree. Some of us need to plant new fruit trees that won't bloom in our lifetimes. Consider this description of early ministry in the interior of Africa by the Congo Bololo Mission:

> Of the first thirty-five CBM missionaries to go to Congo . . . twelve gave their lives in their first year of service, and twelve in their second and third. More remarkable is the fact that in the face of these grim statistics, volunteers continued to pour into Africa in a suicidal stream. Gustav Haupt . . . wrote of his fallen comrades, "They are buried stones for the future building of God."[38]

Overall, of the early pioneering missionaries to Africa, 50 to 90 percent either died or were forced to return home due to sickness.[39] Most of these faithful servants saw little fruit from their ministries. Nevertheless, their sacrifice was not in vain. The *World Christian Encyclopedia* notes that today, "In many ways Africa is hailed as the 'success story' of World Christianity, growing from 9 percent Christian in 1900 to 49 percent in 2020. The Democratic Republic of the Congo is the most profound, rising from 1 percent to 95 percent over that same period."[40] God has built a great monument to His glory with those buried stones. While our missions forefathers had their issues and made their share of mistakes, we have much to learn from their determination and sacrifice.

We modern Westerners like to quantify tasks, make lists, set measurable goals, produce reports, and implement data-driven plans. Missiologists from the Global South refer to this as "managerial missions." To them, our approach can seem rather impersonal and lacking in spiritual nuance. At the same time, we can get frustrated by their apparent lack of structure and follow-through.

A few decades ago, Western and Global South leaders made a goal together: "a church for every people and the gospel for every person by the year 2000." It catalyzed a lot of ministry, but the year 2000 arrived with the Great Commission still incomplete. Missions leaders then started casting vision for 2020. Now, various groups have issued a rallying cry to fulfill the Great Commission by 2033, two thousand years after our Lord Jesus assigned it to His disciples. I respect these initiatives. A lot of good things have happened in the process and many people were engaged who might otherwise have dozed on the sidelines. Being organized and making goals is good, as long as we keep the big picture in mind, maintain a humble posture, remain prayerful, and do not get discouraged if God's timeline does not match ours. We can't reduce the greatest undertaking in the history of the universe to a checklist and a schedule.

> "I think it's difficult and maybe even a little misleading to try and qualify or quantify missionary impact. How can we know what happens to the seeds that are planted?"
>
> ~ CHURCH MEMBER ~

How we define Great Commission "success" has a significant bearing on how we conduct our work. For example, is our goal to have a handful of believers, or to see a significant number of contextualized, multiplying churches? These answers may sound similar, but they can lead us down different paths. Years ago, a new missionary team in Southeast Asia, still in their first year or two of language learning, came up with a ministry plan. Rather than plant a church locally, the team would raise funds to send individuals from the unreached group to the US and set up homestay arrangements for them with members of their home church. They hoped that some would be saved in the process and return to evangelize their homeland. It was a creative idea, but how likely was it really to lead to mature indigenous disciples? I urged the team to sink their linguistic, cultural, and relational roots a little deeper before settling on a church planting strategy.

There is more to world missions than how many converts we can count. The goal of the Great Commission is the glory of God, which comes through the redemption of the nations, but also through the faithfulness of God's people in the process, particularly as they encounter hardship and persecution. The *process* of redeeming the world, not just the result, brings glory to God. When our team first got started among an unreached Muslim group in Indonesia, we dreamed of the progress we would make in ten years. We were devoted, energetic, and committed to seeing multiplying churches form. We did see encouraging progress over that first decade, but the cultural and spiritual challenges were far greater than we anticipated. We started to realize this would be a long process. Thirty years later, the story is still unfolding as the number of churches and disciplers continues to grow. We wish it were happening faster, but trust that God is at work.

DO IT ANYWAY

Whether we find ourselves encouraged or discouraged (or both!) by the present status and momentum of global missions, our bottom-line responsibility is to faithfully pursue the work that Jesus has given us. Our job is to be the best stewards of our lives and resources that we can be. If you see missions being done poorly, plunge in and help. Don't yield to cynicism or apathy.

When faced with a $6 million payment on their campus in

Pasadena, Dr. Ralph Winter, the founder of the US Center for World Mission (now called Frontier Ventures), commented,

> I've never had an overwhelming conviction that this would succeed. What I have had is the overwhelming conviction that it was worth trying. A crucial decision for me before I came was whether I was willing to fail. Was the project valuable enough in the Lord's economy that I was willing to fail? If the whole thing collapses, we hope it will make a real big splash.[41]

I want to make clear that I'm not dismissing the need for excellence in our missions endeavors. We need to practice rigorous thinking, good strategy, informed missiology, and mutual accountability. The task is too important for us to be sloppy. But it is also too important for us to give up because we aren't doing it perfectly. When it comes to obeying God's command to disciple the nations, failure is better than apathy or disobedience. And even "failure" will be temporary because we already know the final outcome is secure.

> **"This perception tends to be more of an excuse among those who are not biblically oriented to remain uninvolved than a heartfelt conviction."**
>
> ~ CHURCH LEADER ~

THE BOTTOM LINE

We are extremely privileged to live in this era of redemptive history. The prophets of old longed to see and hear the things we observe today (Matt. 13:17). Despite many challenges and much satanic opposition, the gospel of Christ is advancing all around the world. Let's be "alert and of sober mind" (1 Peter

5:8), avoiding the temptation toward either triumphalism or defeatism. Don't let the enemy sideline you with discouragement or lure you away with promises of quick and juicy carrots. The Great Commission is a multigenerational, God-sized task. Because He is the Lord of the harvest, world evangelization is in good hands.

God has redeemed untold millions of souls from thousands of sociolinguistic people groups, and He isn't finished yet. His throne room is already teeming with saints. The number and diversity of worshipers grows every day. Missions will not fail because God will not fail. He has a way for each of us to contribute toward the victory He has already won. We glorify God when we seek ways to be more faithful and fruitful. We must walk in step with the Holy Spirit and in loving partnership with one another as we wait for Jesus to fulfill His promise: "I will build my church, and the gates of Hades will not overcome it" (Matt. 16:18).

DISCUSSION QUESTIONS

1. What encourages and discourages you about the church's progress in global missions?

2. Do you find the distinction between Christianity and evangelical believers to be helpful as you read statistics?

3. Do you find it more motivating to think about how much Great Commission work has already been accomplished, or to think about the remaining needs of the unreached?

9

A WAY FORWARD

To know the will of God, we need an
open Bible and an open map.

— WILLIAM CAREY

Back in 2001, not far from where I live in Florida, an antique dealer named Kevin Quinlan bought an Early American–style mahogany card table at an estate sale. He offered $1,650 for it because it was in good condition, although the immaculate finish indicated it was a modern reproduction, not actually an antique from the eighteenth century. It turns out, however, that some things that seem too good to be true can still be true. Quinlan's new card table was soon validated as an original, perfectly preserved Chippendale masterpiece from the mid-1700s. Two weeks after the estate sale, it sold at auction for $1.3 million.[1]

When I read about Quinlan's discovery in the newspaper I began to wonder about the other characters in the story. The owner of the table probably never realized what a treasure she had in her living room. If she did know, she certainly didn't tell her heirs! I wonder if they read the same article I did and realized their oversight. They weren't alone, either. At least a hundred antique dealers besides Quinlan walked by that table at the estate sale, concluded that it was only a copy, and missed out on the biggest return on investment opportunity of their lives. Had they known the table's value, they would certainly have offered a lot more than $1,650 for it.

As Christians, we have been entrusted with something far more valuable than any antique. We have the words of life that provide redemption and salvation for anyone who believes. Kevin Quinlan only had one Early American card table and he had to sell it to receive any benefit from it. When we give the gospel to others, it multiplies.

The accelerating pace of global change requires that the North American church recalibrate our global missions involvement. We need to reevaluate our roles and strategies in light of the dramatic shift in the makeup of the global church, but let's not misinterpret that as an opportunity to opt out. There has never been a more exciting time to be involved in world missions. The first and last laps of a race are the most exciting. While we don't know how much longer we have to run, God has given us the marvelous privilege of witnessing what feel like the "last laps" of the Great Commission race.

At the 1968 Olympics, thousands of spectators remained at the marathon finish line long after the medals were won and the sun went down. They were waiting for John Stephen Akhwari, a runner from Nigeria, who had been badly injured but refused to quit. Of the seventy-five competitors who started the race, eighteen had dropped out. Akhwari explained why he didn't join them: "My country did not send me five thousand miles to start the race. They sent me five thousand miles to finish the race." More than an hour after the winners had finished, the crowds cheered him across the line in the dark. "He was a good runner," one article concluded, "but his performance, courage and dedication in the face of adversity is what history will remember him for."[2]

May we each show the same determination to finish our portion of the race well, regardless of the challenges we face or how many others drop out or race by us. Some of the church's current challenges are the result of centuries of successful missionary efforts. We have helped to build a global body that is now mobilizing for the task, leading us into an era of dynamic partnership. Let's build on that momentum, not fritter our inheritance away at a hasty estate sale.

WAYS TO ENGAGE

When I have opportunities to talk with non-Western leaders of churches and missions movements, I like to ask them how they see the role of Western missionaries in today's globalizing world. What contributions can we make? Very few Global South leaders say that Westerners shouldn't go to the unreached. They simply say it is most helpful if we go with a humble posture and participate in ways that add constructively to, rather than distract from, the work at hand. The responses I have collected over the years can be grouped into five broad functions in which Western missionaries can meaningfully serve the global church: Encourager, Catalyst, Connector, Resourcer, and Pioneer. This is not an exhaustive list, and the roles are certainly not exclusive to Westerners, but we are often particularly primed for these roles based on our cultural values, upbringing, and education.

ENCOURAGER. The impact of encouragement on the church and on global missions is no less significant for being hard to measure. Barnabas, the "Son of Encouragement," played a powerful role in the expansion of the early church into the Gentile world. Paul always affirmed whatever he could in the churches he wrote to. Even his letters to the immature Corinthian believers contain sincere praise alongside pointed critique. The Lord Jesus encouraged as well as corrected in His letters to the seven churches (for example, Rev. 2:2–6) and on many other occasions.

Encouragement comes in many forms—by spoken and written words, presence, friendship, respect, empathy, or a listening ear. My wife and I are now twenty-five years removed from our on-site ministry in Indonesia, but we still have friends who seek us out for counsel because they value our encouragement from a distance. Encouraging colaborers from other nations is a significant part of our investment in global missions.

CATALYST. Every culture has highly artistic, creative, and capable people, but many cultures emphasize continuity more than innovation. "Rocking the boat" is often discouraged, especially for young people. Here's where Westerners can help. Generally speaking, we are raised to ask questions and think outside the box. While that mindset has its downsides, critical thinking can help us navigate change. The pastor of a large church in the Global South once told me, "You Westerners come up with ideas that we wouldn't have thought of, or that we would've been embarrassed to mention for fear that others might think it's a terrible idea. You just plunge in and don't care if someone pushes back." Sometimes, he explained, it's helpful to have a Westerner stimulate conversation, even if their ideas don't always hold much water.

CONNECTOR. Western missionaries are wired to network. Our ability to connect people and resources on a global scale may not be as critical in the future as technology equalizes opportunities to interact, but for now, our networking skills can benefit the global church. We like to set up conferences, think tanks, and cooperative partnerships. We have our fingerprints on much of missions history, which gives us vast data archives and a lot of institutional memory. Mission agencies, in particular, have a rich history of partnerships and collaboration. They are depositories of significant ministry and cross-cultural experience.

RESOURCER. When it comes to contributing resources, we tend to think of money first. The Western church remains very wealthy by global standards and generous stewardship of our funds can make a big impact. However, we have more than money to contribute. The Western world also has tremendous training and educational resources including literature, seminaries, courses, technology, mobile apps, and experience in linguistics, translation, and missiology. These resources can bless the global church for generations to come.

PIONEER. Westerners like pioneering, and American culture particularly celebrates this value. We are can-do people. Access to the frontiers of the unreached is influenced both by globalization and shifting political winds, but in some places, Westerners find it easier to secure visas and jobs, particularly in education and business, than our brothers and sisters from the Global South. A lot of people groups are still unreached, and even once all of them have been engaged for the first time, the church will still have a lot of pioneering missionary work left to do.

Once again, none of these roles is exclusive to Westerners. People from other cultures do all of these things in the missions context and do them well. As individuals, we also have different giftings, so not all Westerners will resonate with the characteristics I have described above. My intention is to provide examples of how North American Christians can have a Great Commission impact, not to limit our options. And let's not forget that we have significant weaknesses as well as strengths. Westerners are not often complimented for our willingness to live sacrificially or to attend all-night prayer vigils. We sometimes lack cross-cultural and language-learning acumen. We are not the greatest at suffering for the gospel and tend to flee the country when danger threatens, if not due to our own fears, then out of concern for

our children, in response to the pleas of loved ones and sending churches, or to avoid legal complications. There are certainly
aspects of missions work in which believers from other cultures
excel more than we do.

Every culture has strengths to contribute to God's great harvest. However, it's not just about what we *give*, but also what we
receive through participation in the Great Commission. When
God calls a few Christians to go, the many who send them are
also blessed. An outward focus expands our hearts, minds, and
the effectiveness of our churches—especially as the unreached
come to our towns and communities. As our society changes,
more and more missionary skills are needed in the West. When
we're connected to worlds outside our own, linking arms with
Christ followers from other cultures, our spiritual journey is en-
riched. We experience a small taste of heaven.

VALUES TO GUIDE US

Management guru Peter Drucker is often credited with saying,
"Culture eats strategy for breakfast."[3] In missions, as in other
areas of life, it's not just a matter of the roles and strategies that
we employ, but also the assumptions and values that undergird
our involvement. I'd like to suggest four values to bolster and
direct our missionary commitment and impact.

Biblical, not expedient. As followers of Jesus, we engage in
missions not because it's convenient or enjoyable, but because we
know it pleases God. His Word teaches us how to honor and obey
Him, and we are to teach others to do the same. The Savior gave
His life for the world, and we now have the privilege of being the

news-bearers, the people with "beautiful" feet who proclaim His goodness in every corner of the globe (Isa. 52:7). As Jesus was sent from His world into ours, so He now sends His church to cultures not our own. We should be willing to take risks and pay a high cost, including our lives, to fulfill our mission. We know that Christ has not left us alone. He promised to be with us as we go, and He has given us the Holy Spirit to lead us into all truth and empower us for His great redemptive purposes.

Collaborative, not mercenary. We have the tremendous joy today of participating in a global effort with a global workforce. Cross-cultural partnership in gospel enterprise is nothing new. The church has been doing it since the first century. What *is* relatively new is the current scale and ease of this collaboration. Most local churches now have access to believers and resources from almost anywhere else in the world. Our brothers and sisters from Asia, Africa, Latin America, and the Pacific are eagerly joining in the task of completing the Great Commission, which represents massive potential for gospel advancement. They have a deep love for the Lord and passion for His glory. They are willing to pay a personal price that many Westerners are not. Our intention should not be to outsource our Great Commission responsibilities, but rather to labor shoulder-to-shoulder with one another in love and with a shared sense of urgency.

> "We need more of the 'everyone to everywhere' mentality and need to do a better job of showing how sending and receiving is part of God's design for healthy churches."
>
> ~ MISSIONARY ~

Strategic, not cheap. Good stewardship is essential, and all of us have very real budget limitations. However, being strategic in our global missions involvement is more important than finding the least expensive route. Winning a war sometimes requires expensive equipment and costly initiatives. All of us need to pray for wisdom in how to best apply the resources God provides. The answers are not easy, and they may be quite different from one church or individual to another. But our goal is the same: to multiply the gospel seed that God has given. As the church grows worldwide, our workforce, funding base, and innovation potential also grow.

Creative, not passive. One of the greatest threats to mission advancement is simply a lack of motivation and intentionality. How passionate are we about the lostness of hundreds of millions of people around us? How often are we gripped with a sense of urgency to reach them? Some of the most effective resources God gives the church are intangible, like our creative ideas, our relationship networks, and our heartfelt prayers. None of those are likely to be tapped without a sense of biblical calling to gospel proclamation. I pray that much of the potential springing from the hearts and gifts of God's people will be channeled into reaching the nations for Christ.

OTHER TASTY CARROTS

The topics covered in this book are not the only misperceptions hindering the North American church's involvement in the mission God has given us. I have encountered a number of other perceptions that have a similar effect, many of which were also mentioned by our survey respondents.

Are people really lost? Fundamental convictions about heaven, hell, and the need for salvation have a significant (but perhaps subconscious) impact on Christians' behavior and motivation, especially for gospel proclamation. According to a Pew study in 2008, a slight majority of American Christians believed that other religions could lead to eternal life.[4] Why share Christ in difficult places if the local people will be fine without Him?

Aren't the needs just as great right here where I live? The growing societal rifts and challenges here at home seem to cry out for more and more of our attention. We have no business going overseas, some suggest, until we've taken the plank out of our own eye and solved the issues in our home communities.

Aren't our methods inefficient and outdated? Missions organizations, in particular, can seem like an inconvenience. Some Christians even feel they're unbiblical and that if the local church were doing its job, agencies wouldn't exist. The overhead cost of sending structures can feel burdensome.

Don't missionaries break the law? Many unreached peoples live in countries that have laws against evangelism and certainly don't offer missionary visas. If that's the case, what are we doing there? And what about missionaries operating as businesspeople, teachers, or aid workers? Are they being deceptive? Access issues are tricky.

Don't I have a right to be safe? It may seem irresponsible to venture into the unknown yourself, much less to "force" such a life on your children, who have little real say in the matter. Our culture places an increasingly high premium on personal safety. We tend to assume we are safer at home than anywhere else in God's world.

These are just a sampling of the questions and doubts that can distract us from our mission or keep us from realizing our full potential. Sun Tzu, a fifth century BC Chinese military strategist, famously said, "The supreme art of war is to subdue the enemy without fighting."[5] If the enemy of the gospel can keep us from recognizing the nature of the battle we are in and the privilege of our God-given role, then he has taken us out of the fight without ever firing a shot. We play into his plans when we allow our sense of urgency about the lostness of human souls and their eternal destiny to fade away.

On your journey with God, and as you help others to understand the big picture of His redemptive plan, try to identify which perceptions are hindering your engagement in the Great Commission and examine them in light of His Word. Don't miss out on your calling in Christ. Carrots are good in hummus and cake, but don't use them to plan your life. Especially not when you have radar.

THE BOTTOM LINE

In Matthew 22, Jesus tells the parable of a great wedding feast. The king has spared no expense for the magnificent gala—his son is getting married! Three times he sends out his servants with invitations, but most of them are turned down by people who are too busy to attend the festivities. Some of the would-be guests even abuse the invitation-bearers. In this story you and I are recipients of the invitation to the king's wedding feast. What an incredible honor! But then we get a second blessing. We are also the privileged servants who, along with the prophets of old, distribute the king's invitations in the streets, calling others to come and celebrate with us.

The key question for believers in the West is not *Should we play a part in global missions?* but *What part in global missions should we play?* How can we make sure that the invitations make it to everyone, everywhere? There are important roles that we from the West are particularly well suited to play, especially as Encouragers, Catalysts, Connectors, Resourcers, and Pioneers. We must fulfill these roles not only with the right strategies, but also with the right attitudes. We must be *biblical, collaborative, strategic,* and *creative.* The global church desperately needs and wants our continued involvement.

God's great banquet hall will eventually be filled with people that most of us would not have expected to attend such an event. They will come from all over the world and celebrate the marriage of the Son in every language. It's going to be a truly spectacular party. Maybe the Europeans will get us all organized so the Pacific Islanders can teach us how to dance!

DISCUSSION QUESTIONS

1. How do you think Westerners can best contribute to world missions?

2. Do any other "tasty carrots" about missions come to mind?

3. Reflecting on this book, what misperception do you think has the biggest negative impact on you or your church?

DON'T FALL FOR THE CON

There is no neutral ground in the universe:
every square inch, every split second, is claimed by God
and counterclaimed by Satan.

—C. S. LEWIS

The Eiffel Tower opened in 1889 as the centerpiece of the Paris World's Fair. It stood almost a thousand feet high and remained the tallest building in the world for more than four decades. It was never intended to last that long, however. The Eiffel Tower was supposed to be dismantled after just twenty years. The French government canceled the 1909 demolition plans after discovering that the Tower made an excellent telegraph transmitter. They used it to communicate with ships in the Atlantic and to intercept German communications during World War I.[1]

The French public fell in love with the Eiffel Tower for a different reason: it democratized the view. Before the Tower, the only way to see Paris from such a height was by hot air balloon, and only the very wealthy could afford that experience. Tickets to climb the Eiffel Tower were cheap enough that common people could admire the skyline and locate their neighborhoods in the broad panorama of metropolitan Paris. The Tower became so important to Parisians that when the Germans occupied the city during World War II, the French Resistance cut the elevator cables to ensure that if German officers wanted to enjoy the view, they'd have to climb the stairs.[2]

The Great Commission provides the same advantages for Christians as the Eiffel Tower did for the French government and residents of Paris. It connects us with the global body of Christ, uniting us in one purpose: the discipleship of the nations. It also reveals a panoramic view of God's redemptive plan for the world across history, allowing us each to find our individual purpose on a global and eternal scale.

> "The Lord of the harvest has a role for every obedient believer to play. That role may change over time, but it is vital for us to engage in the ways God brings to hand as an act of worship."
>
> ~ MISSIONARY ~

In May 1925, a Paris newspaper ran an article about how the Eiffel Tower was beginning to rust and needed extensive repair. Soon after, five of the most prominent scrap iron dealers in Paris received a letter signed by Victor Lustig, Deputy Director General of the *Ministère de Postes et Télégraphes*. Repairing the Eiffel Tower would be extremely costly, Lustig explained, and so the government had reluctantly decided to sell the seven-thousand-ton iron structure for scrap. Lustig arranged a meeting with the metal dealers at a respected hotel to take bids. He emphasized that the plans had to be kept secret because the public would likely protest the dismantling of the Tower.

Like many unscrupulous government officials, Lustig asked one of the bidders, André Poisson, for a substantial bribe to secure the contract. Poisson obliged. Very soon after the money changed hands, he discovered the catch in the seemingly lucrative deal: Victor Lustig was not who he claimed to be. He wasn't even French. Victor Lustig was a con man. His story was plausible enough, and his performance convincing enough, that he sold the Eiffel Tower to a second scrap dealer six months later. Poisson had been too embarrassed to report the scam to the police.[3]

God is not going to allow the global redemption plan that cost His Son's life to fail any more than Paris is going to sell its beloved Eiffel Tower for scrap. But that doesn't stop our enemy from doing all he can to sabotage the Great Commission. His strategies include distraction, deception, and the distortion of God's revealed will. He'd like to sell you some scrap metal that doesn't belong to him and isn't for sale. Don't fall for the con. Especially not more than once.

The most important thing happening in the world today is the advance of the gospel to the ends of the earth by the power of the Holy Spirit. God is preparing the global church as a bride for the Son He loves, and we have the great privilege of participating in that process. The gospel is intended for the whole world, and the Great Commission is for all of us who know Christ. Every Christian should understand God's big-picture plan for redeeming the peoples of the earth and find their place within the worldwide harvest efforts.

In this book we have explored some of the perceptions that discourage the church from wholehearted involvement in God's global redemptive plan, pointing out how each one is unbalanced, simplistic, or built on faulty assumptions. Missions is God's idea, not ours, and it is the central theme of what He is doing in the world, not an optional side project. Western missionaries are not obsolete. Missions is about cross-cultural discipleship, not just any good deed, but it doesn't have to limit or compete against other forms of ministry. Discipleship is a long-term process that can be enhanced, but not replaced, by short-term trips. Missions is for everyone, not just misfits and super-saints. It doesn't harm the cultures God intends to redeem, and it isn't failing. The work of faithful missionaries and the multitude of believers who pray for and support them is having a profound world-wide impact. If we fall prey to apathy, distraction, disobedience, or incompetence, we will be the poorer for it, but the promises and purposes of God will still ultimately prevail.

> "You can't improve on the gospel, which should be our greatest motivator when it comes to the Great Commission."
>
> ~ CHURCH LEADER ~

In Revelation 5, the apostle John stands in the throne room of God and weeps because no one in heaven or on earth can open the scroll whose seals contain judgments on the world. John is comforted when the elders and living creatures fall down to worship Jesus, the Lamb, who is worthy to open the scroll because He was slain to purchase "persons from every tribe and language and people and nation" (Rev. 5:9). The emphasis of their praise is not just that Christ has redeemed a lot of people, but that those people represent the full spectrum of humanity. One day we will celebrate the fulfillment of God's promise to Abraham, "all peoples on earth will be blessed through you" (Gen. 12:3). The global redemption mission will then finally be accomplished, against all odds and at great cost.

We, the church, have the honor of being the instrument through which Christ is demonstrating His mercy, His love, and

His authority to judge the world. He invites and commands us to carry the message of salvation to all of the tribes and peoples and nations who will one day worship side by side with us. Let's respond with faith, with conviction, and with joy, giving our lives in relentless pursuit of the glory of the One who died for us. Our Commission is great because our God is worthy.

ACKNOWLEDGMENTS

The creation of this book illustrates some of the core values we hold dear at Pioneers: a passion for the glory of God in the content, teamwork in the research and writing, innovation and flexibility through the challenges, and an ethos of grace from draft to draft.

I owe a special debt of gratitude to Maxine McDonald for weaving the survey insights, illustrations, and content together. Her contribution would be hard to overstate and we've made a wonderful team.

I am also very grateful to the church leaders, church members, and missionaries who contributed through their survey responses; to Matt Green for his encouragement and editorial help; and to the test readers whose feedback on early drafts informed the material and confirmed the topics. Finally, I deeply appreciate Drew Dyck, Andrew Spencer, and Moody Publishers for championing and refining this book. The whole process has been a joy.

NOTES

Introduction: Why Carrots Aren't Enough

1. K. Annabelle Smith, "A WWII Propaganda Campaign Popularized the Myth That Carrots Help You See in the Dark," *Smithsonian Magazine*, August 13, 2013, https://www.smithsonianmag.com/arts-culture/a-wwii-propaganda-campaign-popularized-the-myth-that-carrots-help-you-see-in-the-dark-28812484/.

2. Anne Ewbank, "Why Wartime England Thought Carrots Could Give You Night Vision," *Atlas Obscura*, October 25, 2017, https://www.atlasobscura.com/articles/carrots-eyesight-world-war-ii-propaganda-england.

Chapter 1: Missions Is Peripheral

Epigraph: F. Lionel Young III, *World Christianity and the Unfinished Task: A Very Short Introduction* (Eugene, OR: Cascade Books, 2021), 92.

1. Ken Curtis, "Whatever Happened to the Twelve Apostles?," Christianity.com, April 28, 2010, https://www.christianity.com/church/church-history/timeline/1-300/whatever-happened-to-the-twelve-apostles-11629558.html.

2. 1 Clement 5:6–7 in *The Apostolic Fathers in English*, 3rd ed., ed. and trans. Michael W. Holmes (Grand Rapids, MI: Baker Academic, 2006), 45.

3. Chris Tomasson, "Vikings: 50 Years Later, Jim Marshall's Wrong-Way Run Remains an NFL Classic," TwinCities.com *Pioneer Press*, October 17, 2014, https://www.twincities.com/2014/10/17/vikings-50-years-later-jim-marshalls-wrong-way-run-remains-an-nfl-classic/amp/.

4. "Jim Marshall's 'Wrong Way Run,'" NFL.com, accessed November 30, 2021, https://www.nfl.com/100/originals/100-greatest/plays-54.

5. Quoted in Juan V. Esteller, "The Secular Life at Harvard," *Harvard Crimson*, January 19, 2016, https://www.thecrimson.com/article/2016/1/19/secular-harvard-esteller/.

6. Peter Greer and Chris Horst, *Mission Drift: The Unspoken Crisis Facing Leaders, Charities, and Churches* (Bloomington, MN: Bethany House, 2014), 16–18.

Chapter 2: Western Missionaries Are Obsolete

Epigraph: Robert Sinker, *Memorials of the Honorable Ion Keith-Falconer, M.A.* (London: George Bell & Sons, 1890), 191.

1. Simon Sinek, *The Infinite Game* (New York: Portfolio/Penguin Random House, 2019), 6–11, Kindle.

2. Gina A. Zurlo and Todd M. Johnson, "Is Christianity Shrinking or Shifting?," *Lausanne Global Analysis* 10, no. 2 (March 2021), https://www .lausanne.org/content/lga/2021-03/is-christianity-shrinking-or-shifting.

3. Todd M. Johnson, "Evangelicals Worldwide," Gordon Conwell Theological Seminary, March 25, 2020, excerpt from the *World Christian Encyclopedia*, 3rd ed. by Todd M. Johnson and Gina A. Zurlo (United Kingdom: Edinburgh University Press, 2019), https://www.gordonconwell.edu/blog /evangelicals-worldwide/.

4. Ibid.

5. Gina A. Zurlo, "The World as 100 Christians," Gordon Conwell Theological Seminary, January 29, 2020, https://www.gordonconwell.edu /blog/100christians/.

6. Mark A. Noll, *The New Shape of World Christianity: How American Experience Reflects Global Faith* (Downers Grove, IL: IVP Academic, 2009), chap. 2, sec. 1, Kindle.

7. C. Gordon Olson, *What in the World Is God Doing?: Essentials of Global Missions: An Introductory Guide*, 6th ed. (Forest, VA: Branches Publications, 2012), chap. 11, sec. 4, Kindle.

8. Jason Mandryk, *Operation World,* 7th ed. (Colorado Springs: Biblica Publishing, 2010), 949.

9. Olson, *What in the World Is God Doing?*, chap. 20, Kindle.

10. Mandryk, *Operation World*, 81.

11. Ibid., 345.

12. Nilay Saiya, "Proof That Political Privilege Is Harmful for Christianity," *Christianity Today,* May 6, 2021, https://www.christianitytoday.com /ct/2021/may-web-only/christian-persecution-political-privilege-growth -decline.html.

13. Mandryk, *Operation World*, 864.

14. "World Migration Report 2020" (Geneva: International Organization for Migration, 2019), 19, https://www.un.org/sites/un2.un.org/files /wmr_2020.pdf.

15. Gus Lubin, "Queens Has More Languages Than Anywhere in the World—Here's Where They're Found," *Insider,* February 15, 2017, https://www.businessinsider.com/queens-languages-map-2017-2.

16. "Toronto's Languages," Endangered Language Alliance Toronto, accessed December 15, 2021, https://elalliance.com/toronto-languages/.

17. Quoted in "Autumn 1942 (Age 68)," International Churchill Society, March 12, 2015, https://winstonchurchill.org/the-life-of-churchill/war-leader/1940-1942/autumn-1942-age-68/.

18. "In U.S., Decline of Christianity Continues at Rapid Pace: An Update on America's Changing Religious Landscape," Pew Research Center, October 17, 2019, https://www.pewforum.org/2019/10/17/in-u-s-decline-of-christianity-continues-at-rapid-pace/.

19. Ralph D. Winter, quoted in "A Wartime Lifestyle" by Doris Haley, *Mission Frontiers*, May 1, 1983, https://www.missionfrontiers.org/issue/article/a-wartime-lifestyle.

20. "Status of Global Christianity, 2022, in the Context of 1900–2050," derived from Gina A. Zurlo, Todd M. Johnson, and Peter F. Crossing, "World Christianity and Religions 2022: A Complicated Relationship," *International Bulletin of Mission Research* 46, no. 1 (January 2022), 71–80, https://www.gordonconwell.edu/center-for-global-christianity/wp-content/uploads/sites/13/2022/01/Status-of-Global-Christianity-2022.pdf.

21. Ibid.

Chapter 3: Everything We Do Is Missions

Epigraph: C. Gordon Olson, *What in the World Is God Doing?: The Essentials of Global Missions: An Introductory Guide*, 5th ed. (Cedar Knolls, NJ: Global Gospel Publishers, 2003), 12.

1. Mary Beth Quirk, "15 Product Trademarks That Have Become Victims of Genericization," *Consumer Reports*, July 19, 2014, https://www.consumerreports.org/consumerist/15-product-trademarks-that-have-become-victims-of-genericization/.

2. "The Origin of the Word 'Yucatan,'" *Yucatan Times,* January 17, 2020, https://www.theyucatantimes.com/2020/01/the-origin-of-the-word-yucatan/.

3. Beth Sagar-Fenton and Lizzy McNeill, "How Many Words Do You Need to Speak a Language?" BBC News, June 24, 2018, https://www.bbc.com/news/world-44569277.

4. "Status of Global Christianity, 2022, in the Context of 1900–2050," derived from Gina A. Zurlo, Todd M. Johnson, and Peter F. Crossing, "World Christianity and Religions 2022: A Complicated Relationship," *International Bulletin of Mission Research* 46, no. 1 (January 2022), 71–80, https://www.gordonconwell.edu/center-for-global-christianity/wp-content/uploads/sites/13/2022/01/Status-of-Global-Christianity-2022.pdf.

5. Robert BG Horowitz, "Attention Rights Holders: The Lessons on Genericism from Thermos Remain Critical," World Trademark Review (April/May 2014), 78–79, https://www.worldtrademarkreview.com/brand-management/attention-rights-holders-lessons-genericism-thermos-remain-critical.

6. *King-Seeley Thermos Co. v. Aladdin Industries, Incorporated,* 321 F.2d 579 (2nd Cir 1963), quoted in "Attention Rights Holders: The Lessons on Genericism from Thermos Remain Critical," by Robert BG Horowitz, World Trademark Review (April/May 2014), 78–79, https://www.worldtrademarkreview.com/brand-management/attention-rights-holders-lessons-genericism-thermos-remain-critical.

7. Quirk, "15 Product Trademarks That Have Become Victims of Genericization."

8. Justia Trademarks, accessed December 9, 2021, https://trademarks.justia.com.

9. Velcro Brand, "Don't Say Velcro," YouTube video, 2:14, September 25, 2017, https://www.youtube.com/watch?v=rRi8LptvFZY.

10. Christopher Little, "The Case for Prioritism," *Transformed from Glory to Glory: Celebrating the Legacy of J. Robertson McQuilkin,* ed. Christopher Little (Fort Washington, PA: CLC Publications, 2015), 177.

11. "Belgian Farmer Accidentally Moves French Border," BBC News, May 4, 2021, https://www.bbc.com/news/world-europe-56978344.

12. Chris Hoffman, "Why Deleted Files Can Be Recovered, and How You Can Prevent It," How-To Geek, June 8, 2018, https://www.howtogeek.com/125521/htg-explains-why-deleted-files-can-be-recovered-and-how-you-can-prevent-it/.

13. J. Campbell White, "The Laymen's Missionary Movement," *Perspectives on the World Christian Movement: A Reader,* rev. ed., eds. Ralph D. Winter and Steven C. Hawthorne (Pasadena, CA: William Carey Library, 1992), 93.

Chapter 4: Missions Competes against Everything Else

Epigraph: Quoted in C. Gordon Olson, *What in the World Is God Doing? The Essentials of Global Missions: An Introductory Guide,* 5th ed. (Cedar Knolls, NJ: Global Gospel Publishers, 2003), 64.

1. Stephen R. Covey, *7 Habits of Highly Effective People: Powerful Lessons in Personal Change,* rev. ed. (New York: Simon & Schuster, 2020), 250, Kindle.

2. Robertson McQuilkin, *Understanding and Applying the Bible: Revised and Expanded* (Chicago: Moody Publishers, 2009), 241.

3. "Roundabouts: An Information Guide" in *National Cooperative Highway Research Program Report 672*, 2nd ed. (Washington, DC: Transportation Research Board, 2010), chap. 1 and 5, https://nacto.org/docs/usdg /nchrprpt672.pdf.

4. "Roundabouts," Issue Briefs #14, US Department of Transportation Federal Highway Administration and the Institute of Transportation Engineers, April 2014.

5. Clint Pumphrey, "How Roundabouts Work," How Stuff Works, accessed December 10, 2021, https://science.howstuffworks.com/engineering /civil/roundabouts.htm.

6. "51% of Churchgoers Don't Know of the Great Commission," Barna Group, March 27, 2018, https://www.barna.com/research/half-church goers-not-heard-great-commission/.

7. Denny Spitters and Matthew Ellison, *When Everything Is Missions* (Orlando: Bottomline Media, 2017), 106–7, Kindle.

8. This quote is widely attributed to St. Francis of Assisi, https://www .christiantoday.com/article/if.necessary.use.words.what.did.francis.of .assisi.really.say/112365.htm.

9. Robertson McQuilkin, "An Evangelical Assessment of Mission Theology of the Kingdom of God," in *The Good News of the Kingdom: Mission Theology for the Third Millennium,* eds. Charles Van Engen, Dean S. Gilliland, and Paul Pierson (Eugene, OR: Wipf & Stock Publishers, 1999), 177.

10. John Piper, in an address at the Lausanne Movement's Cape Town 2010 Congress on October 20, 2010, quoted in "The Church and Other Faiths," accessed January 11, 2022, https://lausanne.org/gatherings /related/the-church-and-other-faiths.

11. Christopher R. Little, "The Case for Prioritism," in *Transformed from Glory to Glory: Celebrating the Legacy of J. Robertson McQuilkin,* ed. Christopher R. Little (Fort Washington, PA: CLC Publications, 2015), 173.

Chapter 5: Missions Is Now Short Term

Epigraph: David Joannes, "Posts Tagged: Journal," davidjoannes.com, accessed March 24, 2022, https://davidjoannes.com/tag/journal/.

1. "Cost of a European Trip – 1910," Gjenvich-Gjonvik Archives, accessed December 10, 2021, https://www.gjenvick.com/OceanTravel/Travel Guide/04-CostOfEuropeanTrip.html.

2. CPI Inflation Calculator, accessed December 15, 2021, https://www .officialdata.org/us/inflation/1910?amount=50.

3. Jean-Paul Rodrigue, "Liner Transatlantic Crossing Times, 1833–1952," *The Geography of Transport Systems*, accessed March 24, 2022, https://

transportgeography.org/contents/chapter1/emergence-of-mechanized-transportation-systems/liner-transatlantic-crossing-time/.

4. "Despite Benefits, Few Americans Have Experienced Short-Term Mission Trips," Barna Group, October 6, 2008, https://www.barna.com/research/despite-benefits-few-americans-have-experienced-short-term-mission-trips/.

5. Robert Wuthnow, *Boundless Faith: The Global Outreach of American Churches* (Berkeley: University of California Press, 2009), 180.

6. Ron Barber, Jr., "Host-Directed Short-Term Missions: Interviews with Japanese Liaisons," *Missiology: An International Review,* vol. 43, no. 3 (July 2015), 320, https://doi.org/10.1177%2F0091829615581930.

7. Benjamin J. Lough, "A Decade of International Volunteering from the United States, 2004 to 2014," Center for Social Development Research Brief No. 15–18 (St. Louis: Washington University, Center for Social Development, 2015), 3, https://doi.org/10.7936/K7B56J73.

8. Ramon Lull (pseudonym), "There's Nothing Short About Short-Term Missions," Desiring God, February 24, 2014, https://www.desiringgod.org/articles/theres-nothing-short-about-short-term-missions.

9. Arlene Richardson, *Threads: One Family's Unlikely Adventure in Business, Mission and Church Planting* (Orlando: Bottomline Media, 2012).

10. "Despite Benefits, Few Americans Have Experienced Short-Term Mission Trips," Barna.

11. A. T. Pierson, quoted in Joseph F. Conley, *Reflections: Musings of an Old Missionary* (Maitland, FL: Xulon Press, Inc., 2009), 95.

12. Daren Carlson, "Why You Should Consider Canceling Your Short-Term Mission Trips," The Gospel Coalition, June 18, 2012, https://www.thegospelcoalition.org/article/hy-you-should-consider-cancelling-your-short-term-mission-trips/.

13. Ramon Lull (pseudonym), "There's Nothing Short About Short-Term Missions."

Chapter 6: Missionaries Are Holy, Rare, and Strange

Epigraph: William Barclay, *The New Daily Study Bible: The Gospel of Luke* (Louisville, KY: Westminster John Knox Press, 2001), 92.

1. Ruth A. Tucker, *From Jerusalem to Irian Jaya: A Biographical History of Christian Missions* (Grand Rapids, MI: Zondervan, 2004), 311.

Chapter 7: Missions Is Harmful

Epigraph: G. P. Howard, "The Logic of Christian Missions," *The Brethren Evangelist,* vol. 66, no. 12 (Ashland, OH: Brethren Pub. House, 1944), 8.

1. Janet D. Stemwedel, "The Philosophy of Star Trek: Is the Prime Directive Ethical?" *Forbes,* August 20, 2015, https://www.forbes.com /sites/janetstemwedel/2015/08/20/the-philosophy-of-star-trek-is-the -prime-directive-ethical/?sh=37f4e83e2177.

2. *Star Trek: The Animated Series,* season 1, episode 8, "The Magicks of Megas-tu," directed by Hal Sutherland, aired October 27, 1973 on NBC.

3. *Star Trek: The Next Generation,* season 7, episode 13, "Homeward," directed by Alexander Singer, produced by Paramount, aired January 15, 1994.

4. Ibid., season 1, episode 22, "Symbiosis," directed by Win Phelps, produced by Paramount, aired April 16, 1988.

5. "'Go Ye and Preach the Gospel': Five Do and Die," *Life,* January 30, 1956, 10–19.

6. Megan Specia, "American's Death Revives Evangelical Debate Over Extreme Missionary Work," *New York Times,* December 2, 2018, https:// www.nytimes.com/2018/12/02/world/asia/john-chau-missionary-evan gelical.html.

7. Toby Luckhurst, "John Allen Chau: Do Missionaries Help or Harm?" BBC News, November 28, 2018, https://www.bbc.com/news/world -46336355.

8. Caitlin Lowery, Facebook, November 24, 2018, https://www.facebook .com/CaitlinSLow/posts/10100184759767623.

9. Howard Zinn, *A People's History of the United States* (New York: Harper-Collins, 2015), chap. 1, Kindle.

10. *Star Trek: The Next Generation,* season 1, episode 8, "Justice," directed by James L. Conway, produced by Paramount, aired November 7, 1987.

11. *Star Trek: Short Treks,* season 1, episode 6, "Q&A," directed by Mark Pellington, aired October 5, 2019 on CBS All Access.

12. Richard N. Ostling, "The New Missionary," *Time,* December 27, 1982, 10, http://content.time.com/time/subscriber/article/0,33009,923232,00 .html.

13. Orji Sunday, "'They Ensure Each Twin Baby Dies': The Secret Killings in Central Nigeria," *Guardian,* January 19, 2018, https://www.theguardian .com/working-in-development/2018/jan/19/twin-baby-dies-secret -killings-nigeria-remote-communities.

14. The story of how God freed the Sawi from this practice is told in the chapters "The Living Dead" and "The Power of Aumamay" of Don Richardson, *Peace Child: An Unforgettable Story of Primitive Jungle Treachery in the 20th Century* (Grand Rapids, MI: Bethany House, 2005).

15. Don Richardson, "Do Missionaries Destroy Cultures?" in *Perspectives on the World Christian Movement: A Reader,* 4th ed., eds. Ralph D. Winter and Steven C. Hawthorne (Pasadena, CA: William Carey Library, 2009), 1109, Kindle.

16. "Globalization and Culture," United Nations Educational, Scientific and Cultural Organization, accessed August 2, 2021, http://www.unesco.org /new/en/culture/themes/culture-and-development/the-future-we-want -the-role-of-culture/globalization-and-culture/.

17. Thomas C. Oden, *How Africa Shaped the Christian Mind: Rediscovering the African Seedbed of Western Christianity* (Downers Grove, IL: IVP Academic, 2007).

18. C. Gordon Olson, *What in the World Is God Doing?: Essentials of Global Missions: An Introductory Guide,* 6th ed. (Forest, VA: Branches Publications, 2012), chap. 10, sec. 3, Kindle.

19. Andrea Palpant Dilley, "The Surprising Discovery About Those Colonialist, Proselytizing Missionaries," *Christianity Today,* January 8, 2014, https://www.christianitytoday.com/ct/2014/january-february/world -missionaries-made.html.

20. Ibid.

21. Ibid.

22. Norvin Richards, quoted in Jeffrey Mifflin, "Saving a Language," *MIT News,* April 22, 2008, https://www.technologyreview.com/2008/04/22 /220796/saving-a-language/.

23. "Almost Half World's Languages Risk Disappearing, Deputy Secretary-General Warns, Urging Action to Preserve Indigenous Cultures, in Message for Global Observance," United Nations Press Release, August 9, 2019, https://www.un.org/press/en/2019/dsgsm1314.doc.htm.

24. Judith Thurman, "A Loss for Words," *The New Yorker,* March 23, 2005, https://www.newyorker.com/magazine/2015/03/30/a-loss-for-words.

25. Jeffrey Mifflin, "Saving a Language," *MIT News*, April 22, 2008, https:// www.technologyreview.com/2008/04/22/220796/saving-a-language/.

Chapter 8: Missions Is Failing

Epigraph: David Bryant, *In the Gap* (Ventura, CA: Regal Books, 1984), 186.

1. Aaron Teasdal, "The Untold Story of the Boldest Polar Expedition of Modern Times," *National Geographic,* December 24, 2020, https://www .nationalgeographic.com/adventure/article/borge-ousland-mike-horn -epic-journey-across-north-pole.

2. Joshua Project, accessed April 28, 2022, https://joshuaproject.net.

3. "Frontier Unreached Peoples," Joshua Project, accessed August 2, 2021, https://joshuaproject.net/frontier.

4. International Mission Board, "Research Reports," IMB, accessed December 14, 2021, https://www.imb.org/research/reports/.

5. "2021 Scripture Access Statistics," Wycliffe Global Alliance, accessed December 15, 2021, https://www.wycliffe.net/resources/statistics/.

6. Frank Gardner, "Iraq's Christians 'close to extinction,'" BBC News, May 23, 2019, https://www.bbc.com/news/world-middle-east-48333923.

7. Gina A. Zurlo and Todd M. Johnson, "Is Christianity Shrinking or Shifting?," *Lausanne Global Analysis* 10, no. 2 (March 2021), https://www.lausanne.org/content/lga/2021-03/is-christianity-shrinking-or-shifting.

8. Ibid.

9. C. Gordon Olson, *What in the World Is God Doing?: Essentials of Global Missions: An Introductory Guide*, 6th ed. (Forest, VA: Branches Publications, 2012), chap. 4, Kindle.

10. Timothy Tennent, "The Translatability of the Christian Gospel," September 16, 2009, https://timothytennent.com/2009/09/16/the-translatability-of-the-christian-gospel/.

11. Jason Mandryk, *Operation World*, 7th ed. (Colorado Springs: Biblica Publishing, 2010), 3.

12. "Population Growth (Annual %)," The World Bank, accessed August 3, 2021, https://data.worldbank.org/indicator/SP.POP.GROW.

13. Todd M. Johnson, "Evangelicals Worldwide," excerpt from the *World Christian Encyclopedia*, 3rd ed. (United Kingdom: Edinburgh University Press, 2019), https://www.gordonconwell.edu/blog/evangelicals-worldwide/.

14. International Mission Board, "Research Reports."

15. Mandryk, *Operation World*, 33.

16. Ibid., 48.

17. Ibid., 59.

18. Ibid., 75.

19. Joseph F. Conley, *Drumbeats That Changed the World: A History of the Regions Beyond Missionary Union and the West Indies Mission 1873–1999* (Pasadena, CA: William Carey Library, 2000), 297.

20. Mandryk, *Operation World*, 619.

21. Ibid., 680.

22. Ibid., 165.

23. Doug Bandow, "North Korea's War on Christianity: The Globe's Number One Religious Persecutor," *Forbes,* October 31, 2016, https://www.forbes.com/sites/dougbandow/2016/10/31/north-koreas-war-on-christianity-the-globes-number-one-religious-persecutor/?sh=1adba7e456e3.

24. Mark Howard, "The Story of Iran's Church in Two Sentences," The Gospel Coalition, July 30, 2016, https://www.thegospelcoalition.org/article/the-story-of-the-irans-church-in-two-sentences/.

25. Joe Carter, "9 Things You Should Know About Christianity and Communist China," The Gospel Coalition, October 2, 2019, https://www.thegospelcoalition.org/article/9-things-you-should-know-about-christianity-and-communist-china/.

26. Zurlo and Johnson, "Is Christianity Shrinking or Shifting?"

27. "Pray for: People's Republic of China," *Operation World,* accessed April 11, 2022, https://operationworld.org/locations/china-peoples-republic/.

28. Philip Yancey, "God on the Move," September 19, 2016, https://philipyancey.com/god-on-the-move.

29. Finishing the Task, "Global 2020 Update," 19, https://finishingthetask.com/wp-content/uploads/FTT-Global-2020-Update.pdf.

30. "Unreached: 100 Largest," Joshua Project, accessed December 14, 2021, https://joshuaproject.net/unreached/1?s=Population&o=desc.

31. Mandryk, *Operation World,* 2–3.

32. Ibid., 973.

33. Ibid., 958.

34. Ibid., 3.

35. Avery T. Willis, *Indonesian Revival: Why Two Million Came to Christ* (Pasadena, CA: William Carey Library, 1977).

36. Mandryk, *Operation World,* 456.

37. Henry T. Blackaby and Claude V. King, *Experiencing God: How to Live the Full Adventure of Knowing and Doing the Will of God* (Nashville: B&H Publishing Group, 1994), 70.

38. Conley, *Drumbeats that Changed the World,* 76.

39. Olson, *What in the World Is God Doing?,* chap. 17, sec. 2, Kindle.

40. Zurlo and Johnson, "Is Christianity Shrinking or Shifting?"

41. Dr. Ralph Winter as quoted in Doris Haley, "A Wartime Lifestyle" *Mission Frontiers,* May 1, 1983, https://www.missionfrontiers.org/issue/article/a-wartime-lifestyle.

Chapter 9: A Way Forward

Epigraph: Craig Brian Larson and Brian Lowery, *1001 Quotations That Connect: Timeless Wisdom for Preaching, Teaching, and Writing* (Grand Rapids, MI: Zondervan, 2009), 101.

1. Sandra Mathers, "Oviedo Man's Bargain of a Lifetime," *Orlando Sentinel*, September 1, 2001, https://www.orlandosentinel.com/news/os -xpm-2001-09-01-0109010303-story.html.

2. "Marathon Man Akhwari Demonstrates Superhuman Spirit," Olympics .com, October 18, 1968, https://olympics.com/en/news/marathon-man -akhwari-demonstrates-superhuman-spirit.

3. Peter Drucker as attributed by Jacob Engel, "Why Does Culture 'Eat Strategy for Breakfast'?," *Forbes*, November 20, 2018, https://www .forbes.com/sites/forbescoachescouncil/2018/11/20/why-does-culture -eat-strategy-for-breakfast/.

4. "Many Americans Say Other Faiths Can Lead to Eternal Life," Pew Research Center, December 18, 2008, https://www.pewforum.org/2008 /12/18/many-americans-say-other-faiths-can-lead-to-eternal-life/.

5. Eric Jackson, "Sun Tzu's 31 Best Pieces of Leadership Advice," *Forbes*, May 23, 2014, https://www.forbes.com/sites/ericjackson/2014/05/23 /sun-tzus-33-best-pieces-of-leadership-advice/?sh=44ff362e5e5e.

Conclusion: Don't Fall for the Con

Epigraph: C. S. Lewis, *Christian Reflections*, ed. Edward Hooper (Grand Rapids, MI: Eerdmans, 2014), 41.

1. Elizabeth Palermo, "Eiffel Tower: Information & Facts," LiveScience, September 28, 2017, https://www.livescience.com/29391-eiffel-tower .html.

2. History.com Editors, "Eiffel Tower," History, A&E Television Networks, updated June 7, 2019, https://www.history.com/topics/landmarks/eiffel -tower.

3. Bill Demain, "Smooth Operator: How Con Man 'Count' Victor Lustig Sold the Eiffel Tower—Twice," *Mental Floss*, August 21, 2020, https:// www.mentalfloss.com/article/12809/smooth-operator-how-victor-lustig -sold-eiffel-tower.

Want to share what you've learned with others?

Pioneers is offering resources for building a Great Commission vision in your church, exclusive bulk book discounts, and a free 10-week small group study that helps readers reflect on and apply the principles found in *Is the Commission Still Great?* This 100% online resource includes videos, discussion questions, a facilitator's guide, and much more.

Get Started!

Pioneers.org/Myths

PIONEERS